T. W. Smith BA

Brodie's Notes on John Milton's

Comus, Samson Agonistes and other Poems

Pan Books London and Sydney

First published 1980 by Pan Books Ltd
Cavaye Place, London SW10 9PG
  2 3 4 5 6 7 8 9
© T. W. Smith 1980
ISBN 0 330 50166 6
Filmset in Great Britain by
Northumberland Press Ltd, Gateshead, Tyne and Wear
Printed by
Richard Clay (The Chaucer Press) Ltd, Bungay, Suffolk

Contents

These Notes are based on the OUP paperback editions of
Comus and other Poems and *Samson Agonistes*, but as careful
line-by-line analysis of the poems and play is given, the
Notes may be used with any edition of these works

To the student

A close reading of the set books is the student's primary task.
These Notes will help to increase your understanding and
appreciation of the poetry and the play, and to stimulate *your own*
thinking about it: *they are in no way intended as a substitute* for a
thorough knowledge of the works.

The author and his work

Milton! thou should'st be living at this hour:
England hath need of thee ...

Thy soul was like a star, and dwelt apart;
Thou hadst a voice whose sound was like the sea
Pure as the naked heavens, majestic, free
So didst thou travel on life's common way,
In cheerful godliness; and yet thy heart
The lowliest duties on herself did lay.
(Wordsworth, *National Independence and Liberty*, Part 1,14 – 180,2–3)

So did a later poetic champion of freedom invoke his predecessor. These two are accepted as our next greatest poets after Shakespeare. Milton and Wordsworth had the same life's ambition: to write a great poem of classical form and inspiring subject matter. Each had the urge of a prophet to warn his fellow countrymen against the decline in moral standards that accompanied political and religious controversy and the desperate combats of a protracted war. Both had high ideals and both were egoists, as is often the case with those having a sense of mission. Milton conducted a verbal campaign against a king and his memory, Wordsworth against an emperor and his conquests.

  John Milton, son of John and Sara Milton, was born on 9 December 1608 in Bread Street, Cheapside, London. He had an elder sister Anne (who married Edward Phillips and had two sons); and a younger brother Christopher, a lawyer. His father had been disinherited for becoming a Protestant, but established himself as a 'scrivener', a kind of attorney, with sufficient means to send his son first to St Paul's School and then on to Cambridge for seven years, where he graduated MA. Thereafter Milton's father supported him for a further five years while he pursued his studies (particularly in poetry and the classics) at the family country home at Horton, Buckinghamshire, close to Windsor Castle. Milton senior, as well as being a kind parent, was a skilled musician; his son inherited some of this talent.

From his Cambridge days onwards John Milton not only prepared to rival Homer and Virgil (in preference to entering the Church as his father wished) but produced occasional pieces that showed great promise. His studies covered the classics, French and Italian, Hebrew and the sciences, including astronomy. He composed poems in Latin and Italian and translated some of the Psalms – 'Let us with a gladsome mind' – at the age of fifteen.

In 1638 Milton set off to see for himself places famous in literature and ancient history, and to make contact with European scholars. He spent over a year in France and Italy but before he could set foot in Greece he felt impelled to return home to play some part in the impending struggle between Parliament and the King. Putting aside his plans to write a great poem, he turned to prose in a series of political and social pamphlets, one result of which was his appointment as 'foreign secretary' (the first man to bear that title): his task was to translate into Latin letters from the government to rulers abroad, and to defend a republican system to a largely monarchical continent. This poetically unproductive period lasted some twenty years. He was wholly dedicated to various causes and did not hesitate to use strong language. His researches – on top of previous years of reading into the small hours – ruined his eyesight; and by 1652, in his forty-fourth year, he was totally blind.

After Milton returned from abroad he lived in London, where he tutored his two now fatherless nephews. In 1643 he suddenly married Mary Powell, a 17-year-old girl half his age a member of a large Royalist family. She left her husband's serious and rather austere household after a month, and it was two years before they were reconciled.

In the meantime Milton had startled – in some cases shocked – readers by a pamphlet recommending divorce for incompatible temperaments. He went on to justify the execution of Charles I in a Latin epistle on behalf of the Council of State for the benefit of foreign powers. When the most highly reputed scholar of the continent Claude de Saumaise (1588–1653) wrote, under the name of 'Salmasius', a defence of the late King Charles, Milton retaliated with *Pro Populo Anglicano contra Salmasium* (1651), in which he gave the aging scholar a drubbing for his bad Latin and poor scholarship and for being influenced by his 'dragon' of a wife! This made

Milton's reputation abroad, and he is said to have come second only to Oliver Cromwell among Englishmen known by name to foreigners. *Pro Populo Anglicano* created an enormous sensation: though it was publicly burnt in a district of Paris, visitors in London from overseas went out of their way to call on Milton. His opponent died while labouring over a reply. Though *Pro Populo* was a convincing victory in the intellectual world, working on it caused the final ruination of its author's eyesight.

Milton had been gradually adapting his life style to his blindness: Most of his work as foreign secretary was tactfully transferred, but he continued to perform some of his duties at a reduced salary; he moved to a house in a quiet part of Westminster, where his nephews helped him with reading and dictation – a family task to be carried on for some years. His daughters, too, assisted with this, though sometimes grudgingly: their ignorance of languages and scholarly names produced irritating errors of pronunciation; but as Milton had regarded scholarship as being outside a woman's sphere this was hardly surprising. He was not an unkind father but he lacked understanding. His first wife had died in 1652 leaving him with three daughters, their little son John having died before he was two. Milton's second wife Katharine Woodcock died in childbirth within a year of their marriage; his third wife Elizabeth Minshull looked after him and long survived him. He used to complain that without his gout his blindness would have been bearable.

Milton's devotion to the Parliamentary cause was the first great obstacle to the fulfilment of his poetic ambitions. The second was his blindness, which diverted him from the fullest exercise of his talent, depriving him of the intellectual refreshment of his library (a number of volumes in which were 'lost'), and blotting out those 'various objects of delight' he had listed so joyously in *L'Allegro* and *Il Penseroso*.

'Thus with the year
Seasons return; but not to me returns
Day, or the sweet approach of even or morn
Or sight of vernal bloom, or summer's rose,
Or flocks, or herds, or human face divine.' (*Paradise Lost*, 3,40)

Milton blamed himself for his 'late spring'; his winter set in early.

Milton recognized the Restoration as the overthrow of the cause for which he had worked in the prime of life with his mental powers at their keenest. He suffered financially, and narrowly escaped execution, for his part in bringing about the subsequently hated Commonwealth. Instead, through the good offices of admirers (some of them Royalists) he was granted 'old age obscure' – though by no means unvisited. In this state he laboured patiently with the composition and dictation (friends joining in taking it down) of twelve books (over ten thousand lines) of *Paradise Lost* (1667), which gained instant praise and placed him where he wished to be: on the same plane as Homer, Virgil and Dante. He received £10 for two instalments; today's equivalent of that sum would of course be vastly greater.

The much shorter *Paradise Regained* (1671) was his response to a young Quaker friend, Thomas Ellwood, who frequently read to him. Finally, having delineated God and Satan, Adam and Eve, the Son of God and the Tempter, as they moved through vast realms and huge landscapes, he created out of the Hebrew chronicles an individual hero on a prison exercise-ground, humiliated, blinded and tainted, with nothing to live for, who snatches victory out of defeat.

During the Great Plague in 1665 Milton stayed with his household in the only surviving Milton dwelling, a cottage at Chalfont St Giles. Back in London the following year he was fortunate that his house narrowly escaped the Great Fire, though he had further financial loss to face in the destruction of his birthplace in Bread Street. Could he have heard the crash of steeples and pictured to himself the collapse of the theatre in Gaza? Did he wonder if this could be some divinely contrived catastrophe for the Philistines of his generation?

John Milton died peacefully on 8 November 1674. He was buried in the chancel of St Giles, Cripplegate, near his father, who had died at the age of eighty-four. Here Cromwell had been married in 1620.

In 1940 St Giles was bombed: the chancel tablet was destroyed and in the churchyard Milton's statue was found with a tin hat on its head and bunch of keys in its hand! His best loved monument, however, is the brick-and-timber cottage in Chalfont St Giles, where he completed *Paradise Lost*. Here is a museum of objects connected with Milton and his time, and to this place come the literary pilgrims, among them admirers from the once distant Americas.

Looking back from the distance of three centuries, we can see how Milton's personal career merged with that of his one dramatic hero: both attained a greater triumph in their blind state than anything performed when they could see. The pamphleteer who weakened his eyesight justifying the ways of England to Europe turned his vision inwards to justify in immortal verse the ways of God to Man.

Further reading

Milton: A Biography, Parker, William Riley (OUP)

Milton: A Structural Reading, Bouchard (Edward Arnold)

Milton: A Collection of Critical Essays, edited by Martz (Prentice-Hall and Spectrum Books)

Milton: A Selection of Critical Essays, edited by Rudrum (Macmillan Modern Judgements Series and Macmillan Papermacs)

Puritanism

The English Puritans were religious and social reformers whose attitude to established forms of worship was similar to that of the Waldensians, a religious movement for voluntary poverty (see Milton's sonnet on the slaughter of one group of them in the Alps: 'On the late Massacre in Piemont'). Like most church reformers they claimed to return to a purity of mind and soul unspoilt by material possessions and ceremonial splendour. Their habit of praying aloud and singing hyms brought ridicule from the worldly, but their intense earnestness and strict discipline made them ultimately a force to be feared in battle. They proved to be the backbone of the Parliamentary army and, financed by the wealth of the City of London, their success against spirited cavaliers, professional troops and even dour Scots and wild Irishmen was assured. Cromwell ruled by virtue of their well-trained infantry, though he had also to cope with much visionary fanaticism. The age was one of endless theological argument (witness much of *The Pilgrim's Progress*, 1678), which not infrequently led to blows.

Milton's own views were subject to change. As a university man he differed little, apart from a natural sobriety, from the general run of his contemporaries. He showed some (inherited) stubbornness to a tutor, over the curriculum, but that was all. But once he had given himself to politics (and he was conscious of the sacrifice), he became progressively rigid in outlook. No doubt his unhappy initiation into married life also hardened his attitude, for the tone of much of his pamphleteering is hectoring and abusive. He recommended divorce based on disagreement, the meting of justice to despots and, in his prose masterpiece *Areopagitica* (1644), the abolition of licences to print. However, like most idealists, Milton found human nature only too ready to abuse freedom and to substitute one tyranny for another. He became antagonistic to the Presbyterians and acquired a strong dislike of the Scots. In his last years he belonged to no sect, nor did he attend any place of worship.

Yet it would be wrong to accept a commonly held view of Milton as a cultured young poet who was turned into a sour sectarian by his experiences. He retained, as we see in two of his sonnets, a quiet love of the social graces. His conversation in his blind state, seated out of doors in a chair or led by a 'guide' on familiar walks, drew regular visits from men of distinction. Throughout his life he was the champion of that nobler form of Puritanism which left its permanent mark on the English character, whose standard in an age of semi-pagan self-indulgence was personal 'virtue', ranging from simple honesty and steady loyalty to the ideal of chastity and the regal glamour of virginity. He wrote in one of his pamphlets: 'He who would not be frustrate of his hope to write well hereafter in laudable things ought himself to be a true poem.' In his case both poet and poetry constitute monuments. To end with a further quotation from Wordsworth, applicable to all generations: 'We must be free or die, who speak the tongue/That Shakespeare spake; the faith and morals hold/Which Milton held' (*National Independence and Liberty*, Part 1,16).

Comus and the minor poems

The classical element

No English poet has drawn more fully in his works on the myths and legends of the ancient Greeks and Romans than Milton. Their poems and dramas provided ample material for enriching native verse with allusions and comparisons to once familiar gods and goddesses, spririts and monsters, satyrs and sirens, heroic adventures and bewitching sorceresses. Supernatural beings, with so many human traits writ large and so many exciting stories linking them together, added colour and depth to the diction with which they were mingled. They are no longer worshipped or feared or imagined down in the forest or up on the mountain, but they largely live on in verse, much of which is immortal and cherished by those reared on it. For generations of Englishmen they remained familiar in adult life, from earlier years spent mastering Latin and Greek grammar; such an education was needed to appreciate fully what we call 'classical allusions'. Today these stories are no longer common ground among writers and readers, except for those who take a special interest in Mythology or the Ancient World.

Notes on references in the text are bound to be limited to the briefest explanation of identities or functions. Fortunately, nearly all can be looked up in the most modest of encyclopedias, and the more specialized provide histories and backgrounds. Many names have by constant usage become part of our vocabulary: jovial, mercurial, tantalize, psychic, titanic, etc. This section is intended as a brief guide to a large and varied world of gods and other creatures who once dominated the consciousness of peoples of 'heathen' religions, primitive superstitions, mingled cults and vivid poetic imaginations. Centuries of conflicting and cross-bred beliefs and ceremonies in that melting-pot of races and civilizations, the Mediterranean world, make a straightforward account impossible. The most important mingling was that of the mythology of the serious-minded rather earthy Italian farmers and soldiers, with the frequently parallel mythology of the Greek mariners and philosophers – lighter and more fanciful in some ways, darker and more mysterious in others. The Jupiter of the Romans became identified with the Greek Zeus in both temples and literature, with similar pairings of other gods, a process facilitated by the extent of the Roman Empire.

In popular belief, as well as poetic imagination, the gods were immortal and moved freely through the universe, sometimes shining as stars or constellations, sometimes descending to earth in disguise as humans or animals. They had spheres of influence, though they were not necessarily all-powerful, as there were rivalries. Some were benefactors whose gifts could be obtained by performing the proper rites; some had the ability to transform a human into a god or even a star – or into the grossest of animals. They often had favourites among humans, while others they pursued with utter hatred. They would watch, with amused detachment from above, the misfortunes of unlucky mortals below. They feasted together on 'ambrosia' and 'nectar', and met occasionally in council. As they clearly had much time on their hands, intrigues developed among the gods themselves; love affairs were frequent, especially with a human of the other sex. The supreme god, *Jupiter* (or Jove), had numerous liaisons with goddesses or pretty nymphs, some of which led to cruel reprisals by his jealous wife Juno. Others were almost equally active, and there are endless variations and contradictory versions, with different local deities or personalities sharing the same name.

Numerous stories and family descents were unblushingly invented by poets and playwrights in the later centuries of the Roman Empire. The ancients saw their own peccadilloes reflected and magnified in those of the divinities, as did later men and women living under the Tudors and Stuarts and devouring pastoral romances. In the seventeenth century Milton had no hesitation in giving *Comus*, the Roman god of revelry, a father in *Bacchus* and a mother in the enchantress *Circe*. It is remarkable that he should have concentrated so intensely on the lives of this irresponsible, amoral world – with its illicit loves and petty quarrels – for a masque actually dedicated to the ideal of chastity!

The main body of the gods is grouped round two generations; *Saturn* and his brother and sister *Titans*, and his son and successor,

Jupiter and *his* brothers and sisters. From various matings of these were descended not only such well-known figures as *Appollo*, *Diana*, *Venus*, *Mars* and *Mercury*, but also the mythical ancestors of Greeks, Trojans, Egyptians and Romans. The Titans were the children of *Uranus* (Sky) and *Gaea* (Earth), who emerged from the primeval Chaos (formless space). Further offspring of this fundamental pair were the three *Cyclops* and other giants. Gaea had more children by *Pontus* (Sea) including the three dreadful *Harpies*, and among her grandchildren were Iris the rainbow messenger, and the three *Gorgons* whose faces could turn beholders to stone. Gaea had by *Tartarus* a whole progeny of monsters, including the *Hydra*, the *Chimera*, and *Cerberus*, the dog-like guardian of the door to the underworld.

The Titans were more human, though still huge by comparison. Eldest was *Oceanus*, who had a large family; the youngest was *Saturn* (Roman) or *Cronos* (Greek), an intriguing character whose two identities have caused confusion. Cronos rescued his fellow Titans from their tyrannical father and was allowed therefore to rule over heaven, provided he reared no male children. Consequently he swallowed his sons at birth, until his wife hid *Zeus* (Jupiter) and his two brothers. Eventually Jupiter supplanted Cronos, who, exiled in Italy where he was known as Saturn, taught mankind agriculture and established a legendary 'Golden Age' – his spirit lives on in our attitude to Saturday as a day for fêtes, and amusements in general.

Jupiter divided the universe by lot with his brothers *Neptune* and *Pluto*. His share was heaven and earth, while Neptune replaced *Oceanus* and Pluto reigned in the underworld. Jupiter had to suppress a revolt by the dispossessed Titans and later by assorted giants, relying on thunderbolts made for him by his son *Vulcan*, born to *Juno*, his queen. As a reward Jupiter gave this misshapen forger of weapons, who worked under volcanic mountains, the lovely *Venus* (his own illegitimate daughter) as a bride. Another son of Jupiter and Juno was *Mars*, god of war (and therefore well provided with arms made by his brother) who had an affair with Venus, from which union came no less a person than *Cupid* (the Greek *Eros*). The one daughter was Hebe, goddess of youth.

Jupiter's other children resulted from excursions he kept as secret as possible from his wife. By Dione he had Venus herself, though by an alternative tradition she was born in sea foam and, coming ashore, was welcomed by the *Hours* (who were the deities of the seasons and themselves children of Jupiter); the Hours took her to their father among the gods. Identified with the Greek Aphrodite and to some extent with the Syrian Astarte, Venus was goddess of love, beauty, laughter and the pleasures of life. By *Maia* Jupiter had *Mercury*, swift messenger and god of commerce. By *Metis* he had *Minerva*, but this goddess of wisdom and the arts was actually born from her father's head.

The famous twins *Apollo* and *Diana* were born to their beautiful mother *Latona*, in the island of Delos. She gave birth to them leaning against a palm tree (see 'Comus', line 355). Her father was a Titan married to *Phoebe* (Greek for 'Bright One', from the radiance of the moon), which name, in the masculine form *Phoebus*, passed to Apollo, god of the sun, who replaced the Titan *Hyperion*. Diana, goddess of hunting and chastity, was similarly called *Phoebe* as goddess of the moon, and *Hecate* as goddess of the underworld – a triple deity. She was also known as *Cynthia* from the mountain in Delos where she was born. As Hecate, she was often identified with *Persephone*, carried off by Pluto. These fluctuating combinations make any attempt at a genealogical tree of the classical gods nearly impossible.

There are several groups of three. In addition to the three dread Gorgons already referred to, there were: the three Graces, born of Venus by Jupiter; the three Fates and the three Hours, born of the Titan *Themis* (Roman goddess of justice) by Jupiter. The worship of the Fates, with their distaff, spindle and scissors controlling the thread of human life, was often mixed up with that of the three Furies, dread ministers of vengeance constantly punishing the guilty. The three Sirens were sired by the eldest son of Oceanus.

In addition to these principalities and powers there were, especially at a local level, innumerable nameless spirits, nymphs of the seas and rivers, the trees and the mountains, fauns (Latin) and satyrs (Greek) grinning through the foliage and terrifying the locals when not in hot pursuit of nymphs. Every bush, every stream was the haunt of one of the latter. Greatest of all nature spirits was the son of Mercury and *Penelope* (before her marriage to *Ulysses*), namely *Pan* (meaning 'all'), with his goat's horns and legs; his Latin name was Faunus.

Perhaps the most popular legends were those involving love

between gods and humans: Apollo's pursuit of the lovely *Daphne* until she was turned into a laurel bush, from which the enamoured god took the now well-worn laurel wreath; Cupid's nightly assignment with the fair *Psyche*, her persecution by his mother Venus, and their reunion by the good offices of the gods in committee; Venus's own obsession with the handsome but unresponsive *Adonis*, who preferred hunting wild animals, died of a boar wound and subsequently was allowed six months in the year for a return to earth (paralleled by, if not originating from, the worship of *Osiris* in Egypt, or that of *Thammuz* in Phoenicia); *Orpheus*, son of Apollo and one of the Muses, and his *Eurydice*, whom he brought back from Pluto's realm of the dead, only to lose her again because he looked back at her before reaching the exit; poor Echo, banished from the gods' presence for talking too much, and losing her heart to Narcissus – too absorbed in his beautiful reflection in the water to pay attention to her – only to turn into an empty shell capable merely of repeating the words she heard.

Another kind of shell was used to calm the waves by the sea god *Triton*, half man and half dolphin, son of Neptune. The monarch of the sea had another son, the fisherman *Glaucus* who, after being transformed into a sea god, fell in love with *Scylla*. Unable to win her he resorted to *Circe* for a love potion, but the sorceress fancied him instead and put poisonous juice into Scylla's fountain when she was bathing. This changed her into an enormous and frightful monster, part of which barked like dogs; Scylla threw herself into the sea and so formed the dangerous rocks opposite the formidable whirlpool *Charybdis*. Sailing between them was a navigational hazard in the days of Ulysses.

All these characters are alluded to somewhere in the poems dealt with in these Notes; others are explained as the occur. What, the student may ask, is the ancestry of *Comus*, son of *Bacchus* and *Circe*? The maiden that Jupiter is said to have loved most of all was *Semele*. Juno disguised herself and persuaded the god to woo her as himself and not in human form. His divinity burned her to death, but Jupiter seized their infant son and gave him to his aunt *Ino* to nurse. This led to Juno's driving the husband of Ino so mad that he attacked her with ferocity. The fair-skinned Ino then threw herself into the sea, becoming the deity *Leucothea*, 'the white goddess'.

Meanwhile Semele's son Bacchus (or *Dionysus*) grew up into a handsome youth, fond of wild festivities, stimulated by the juice of the vines whose cultivation he spread through many lands. His cult was followed by intoxicated disciples, especially women of all ages. The behaviour of the Bacchantes, as they were called, was a kind of religious raving, referred to by the historian of Greece, George Grote (1794–1871), as 'those violent ecstasies and manifestations of temporary frenzy and that clashing of noisy instruments' (not unknown in modern times!). Euripides, Milton's favourite Greek dramatist, represents in his tragedy *The Bacchae* the mass hysteria that induced the mother of King Pentheus to slay him for attempting to prevent the spread of this kind of worship (the madder it was the more infectious it became) in defiance of the god himself. The unfortunate Orpheus, mourning his Eurydice, refused to join these wild women in their orgies and was torn to pieces.

Many stars still bear the names bestowed on them by ancient custom. The Great Bear is derived from *Callisto*, loved by Jupiter, changed into a bear by the jealous Juno, and again by Jupiter into the constellation near the North Pole with two of its stars pointing to the Pole-star. The Greek word for bear, 'arktos', has given us 'Arctic'. The Phoenicians navigated by the present Pole-star in the tail of the Lesser Bear, whereas the Greeks followed Arcturus (meaning 'bear-guard') in the Great Bear. Not far away are Andromeda and the constellation of Cassiopeia. Some confusion is caused by the names given to the planet Venus: in the evening after sunset it was called *Hesperus*, the name of the grandfather of the *Hesperides* who kept a famous garden; in the morning before sunrise its name was *Lucifer*, elsewhere a fallen angel!

The winds had their personal names, of which Zephyrus, the west wind, had left us a pleasant impression in 'zephyr', a gentler breeze than the British 'wild west wind'. The ruler of winds and storms was Aeolus, located in the Aeolian Isles and inventor of sails, as well as an astronomer. Another figure hovering between invisible godhead and historic personality was *Atlas*, at once a Titan and a king of Mauretania. As the first he was punished by Jupiter for helping the giants: Jupiter forced him to hold up the world on his shoulders (hence the figure on volumes of maps, and which has given us the word 'atlas'. As king of Mauretania, Atlas was turned into stone when Perseus held up the Gorgon's head before him. As the tides of Oceanus washed the shores of north-west Africa, that particular sea, the Atlantic, took its name from Atlas.

A further geographical manifestation was the pursuit by the river god *Alphaeus* (in southern Greece) of the nymph *Arethusa*, changed by Diana into a fountain in a Sicilian island – whither Alphaeus followed her. Anything thrown into the river Alphaeus would reappear in the fountain

Certain birds were not always what they appeared to be. The plaintive cries of nightingale and swallow were traced to two sisters, *Philomela* and *Procne*. The latter's husband *Tereus*, King of Thrace, developed a passion for her sister Philomela, and cut off her tongue so that she could not betray him. But Procne found out, and during the festival of Bacchus the two sisters served Tereus's young son as a meal to him. As he drew his sword all three were turned into birds, Tereus joining the hoopoes.

Another sad story is that of *Halcyon* (Greek *Alkuon*, a kingfisher): she and her husband, who had been drowned at sea, were changed into legendary birds that bred in a nest on the sea in midwinter, inducing a fourteen-day spell of calm weather (hence 'halcyon days'). Better known is the fabulous *Phoenix*, of which only one existed, reported by early Greeks from either Arabia or Egypt. After living for five hundred years it was consumed by fire and immediately reborn from its ashes (see 'the secular bird of ages' in *Samson Agonistes* 1699–1707, and *Paradise Lost*, 5,271–4).

Dolphins, today's intelligent acrobats, have been known for their friendliness over the centuries. One carried the well-known Greek musician Arion ashore after he leaped overboard to escape from a piratical crew. Another ill-intentioned crew seized Bacchus when asleep, but the god drove them overboard to become dolphins.

This summary may suitably end with the *Genius*, a spirit that not only inhabited every significant place but was attached to every man from birth, to watch over him. (The Greek word was 'daimon'.) On each man's birthday his Genius was propitiated with flowers, incense and libations of wine. Much later 'genius' came to mean an intellectual gift of a high order. The genius of Milton inspired majestic verse, rich in thought and harmonious in sound, works of art that have helped to keep his country prominent in world literature.

Some topography

The 'Infernal Regions' (from Latin *infernus*, 'lower'), were a comprehensive underworld for all departed 'shades'. If they had been virtuous, in the patriotic sense, on earth, they followed pursuits (like those they had known when alive) in Elysium, a beautiful paradise; others lingered in an intermediate stage in Erebus, where all was dark. The guilty suffered torments in Tartarus, originally the prison for the defeated Titans. According to some, the lovely Garden of the Hesperides was reserved for the guardians of the three golden apples given to Jupiter by Juno on their wedding day; it was believed to lie out in the west somewhere beyond the Atlantic.

It is impossible to give an accurate general description of these other worlds, as changes took place according to religious fashion or poetic fancy. The change in meaning of Hades (Hell) is interesting: originally another name for Pluto, and for his underworld kingdom, it now has the worst sense attached to it. Similarly 'infernal' now means 'hellish'.

What of the Spheres, whose music is mentioned so often? In Plato's *The Republic* a man recovered when given up for dead. Like others on the point of dying, he had visions: he described the great spindle of adament that caused eight concentric spheres to revolve; they were centred on the earth, as in the Ptolemaic system, and were transparent. On each sat a siren, whose single notes together formed a harmony. This phenomenon was invisible and inaudible to humans. The conception became a favourite with poets. Later some philosophers added two more spheres, and one school allotted the seven inner spheres (starting from the earth outwards) to the Moon, Mercury, Venus, the Sun, Mars, Jupiter and Saturn. Then came the eighth sphere, studded with all the fixed stars; the ninth, crystalline; and the tenth the 'primum mobile', a solid outer shell that activated the movement of all the rest. Though Milton knew of the theories of Copernicus, he followed the old Ptolemaic arrangement of the universe in his poetry: Ptolemy was a Greek astronomer of the second century AD.

Earlier style

O Mighty-mouth'd inventor of harmonies,
O skill'd to sing of Time or Eternity,
God-gifted organ-voice of England,
Milton, a name to resound for ages (Tennyson, *Alcaics*, 'Milton', 1863)

In each of these lines, by the Poet Laureate of the second half of the nineteenth century, is a word associated with music. Tennyson was the most musical of poets but he professed awe of Milton's grander harmonies. Their construction was the fruit of early musical training and the mastery of both classical and modern tongues and, of course, years of perfecting his art. He was gifted with, and constantly exercised a discrimination in, sounds and careful distinction in meanings. Vowels are modulated and consonants alliterated for special effects, often modelled on Greek and Latin passages as familiar to him as his native English. In particular, he embarked on elaborate sentence structures as ambitious as anything in the classics, where word-formation made such things more feasible.

The long, involved, periodic sentence was more difficult in English, with its few inflections; Milton often succeeded impressively, but many passages are highly artificial and needlessly cumbered with clauses. In 'At a Solemn Music' line 17 depends on a verb in line 3. In his earlier poems, with the exception of the dialogue in *Comus*, rhyme controls and restrains the soaring imagination which, in the continuous blank verse of the epic poems, unfolds a huge canvas full of pictorial detail and echoing with a variety of sounds. A master of the complex sentence, with its changing rhythms and shifting emphasis, Milton boldly stiffened his metre with frequent inversions – object first, verb last, phrases separated from the words they are attached to – and constant ellipsis of link words: conjunctions, relative pronouns, prepositions. This compacted diction (which reminded many of laborious construing in the Latin set) was condemned as contortion of the language by critics like the learned Dr Johnson, the old Tory who was only too ready to find some, but not every, fault with a Puritan poet.

It has been calculated that Shakespeare's works have the largest vocabulary in English literature with 15,000 words; next to him comes Milton with 8,000. Substantial evidence of this is to be found in the *Shorter Oxford Dictionary*, which provides countless extracts from Milton's works in illustration of definitions, including a very large number of variant or archaic meanings. Some of his choices were indeed consciously archaic at the time, to give antique flavour. He was also an experimenter: it is hardly surprising that 'immixed', 'disglorified' and 'remediless' did not catch on. On the other hand, quite a number of household expressions were, surprisingly, first coined by him: 'dire necessity', 'silver lining', 'dim religious light', 'cricket on the hearth', 'last infirmity of noble minds', 'fresh fields and pastures new', 'more is meant than meets the eye' etc.

In the early poems there is the usual sprinkling of similes and metaphors and other figures of speech, but what catches eye and ear is the varied use of epithets, as well as their profusion. Compound hyphenated epithets are very numerous:

pale-eyed priest	love-darting eyes
empty-vaulted night	amber-dropping hair
low-roosted lark	hard-besetting need
coral-paven bed	leaden-stepping hours

A special arrangement is the Greek balancing of two adjectives, fore and aft:

sad occasion dear	forced finger rude
gloomy covert wide	inferior creatures mute
flocking shadows pale	narrow place enclosed

Hypallage, (by transferring the epithet to a noun to which it does not strictly belong but which is in some way associated with it), vivifies while it condenses; from the person to something inanimate:

shuddering dew	sceptred pall
sainted seat	dolorous mansions
prophetic cell	perplexed paths
pensive scenery	widowed bed

or descriptive epithet applied to an abstract noun:

nodding horror	blear illusion
squint suspicion	swilled insolence
suspicious flight	mortal frailty
retired solitude	chaste austerity

From this it is an easy step to full personification with capital letter and the one sufficient epithet:

brooding Darkness	staid Wisdom
grey-hooded Even	retired Leisure
pure-eyed Faith	lewdly-pampered Luxury
white-handed Hope	wrinkled Care
leprous Sin	spare Temperance

It was this kind of instant creation of a Person out of an idea, a feeling or a condition that plagued the fashionable diction of poets, major and minor, in the eighteenth century. And it was this artificiality against which Wordsworth revolted in favour of simple ballad language. In these earlier poems of Milton's there are few developed personifications like 'thievish Night, with her dark lantern or 'still Morn' with her sandals grey, simply because they are peopled with active beings from classical mythology, whose functions and imagined appearance provided sufficient poetic substance.

Milton employs so much repetition – of name, of epithet or of idea – that there *has* to be a clear purpose in it, and a variety of purpose. There is much in the tenser passages of dialogue in *Samson Agonistes*; in the earlier poems it is less noticeable, apart from the passionate 'For Lycidas is dead, dead ere his prime,/Young Lycidas, and hath not left his peer./Who would not sing for Lycidas?'

There is some tautology, consious or unconscious, in which the meaning is expressed twice for emphasis: 'weeping and loud lament/sage and solemn tunes/utmost end ... and none left out/degenerate and degraded state/less warranted than this or less secure ...'

More frequently there is an effective balance, not of opposites but of similars, in 'even step and musing gait/pert fairies and dapper elves/calling shapes and beckoning shadows/obscure haunts of inmost bowers/unlock the clasping charm and thaw the numbing spell/Hence with denial vain and coy excuse.' The last is also an example of 'chiasmus' (from a Greek letter shaped like a cross), a favourite figure with Milton, in which the second part reverses the order of corresponding parts of speech, e.g. the noun precedes the adjective instead of following it: 'Tomorrow to fresh woods and pastures new.'

Changes of meaning and fashion have made many words obsolete, requiring explanation in notes. Milton uses the following in the sense enclosed in brackets: virtue (manly quality), sentence (opinion), solemnity (festival), artful (skilled), curious (fastidious), which are derived from Latin roots; uncouth (unknown), shrouds (shelters), gear (business), which are native English and sometimes survive in dialect.

Metre

'On the Morning of Christ's Nativity' (1629): Introductory four stanzas of seven *iambic* (the individual foot being two-syllabled, the second accented) lines, six in pentameters (five feet) and the seventh an alexandrine (six feet), rhyming ababbcc. An alexandrine also rounds off each of the twenty-seven stanzas of the Hymn proper, paired for rhyming with the preceding four-foot line. The whole stanza is a bold experiment with lines of varying length and *trochaic* variations: feet 33533546, rhymes aabccbdd. (A *trochee* is a foot of one long syllable followed by one short syllable.)

'On Shakespeare' (1630): Sixteen lines arranged in rhyming couplets, in the manner of many epitaphs inscribed on memorial tablets.

'At a Solemn Music' (?1632): Substantially twenty-eight lines of rhyming couplets broken by occasional short lines and ending with an alexandrine.

'On the New Forcers of Conscience' (1646): This sonnet has an extension observed by Milton among the Italians and inserted by him before the concluding couplet; it consists of two tercets (three-line verses) of 5,5,3.

Comus (1634): Dialogue in blank verse, except Comus's opening invocation, which is in octosyllabic couplets like *L'Allegro* and *Il Penseroso*; the Spirit's appeal to Sabrina and his closing speeches are also in octosyllabic (8–syllabled) couplets, but with a predominance of the lighter trochaic lines (of seven syllables). The songs have a musical setting; that to Echo ends with a long drawn-out alexandrine, like a prolonged echo. Lines 277–90 are an example of Greek 'stichomythia', sharply contrasting single-line speeches.

Arcades (1633): Blank verse and songs.

Lycidas (1637): The irregularity of the metre, pentameters with three-foot lines at intervals, like the sudden breaking of a wave, rhymes uniting and separating, sometimes in couplets, sometimes alternating, sometimes harking back several lines – these are devices suggesting the disordered gestures of passionate mourning or the swelling and subsiding of the surface of the sea. The closing narrative of eight lines rhymes like a stanza: abababcc.

The masque

Masques (or masks) were special entertainments laid on for important occasions, usually in aristocratic surroundings; they competed in spectacular display with the pageants that wound their way through the streets of London (of which the Lord Mayor's Show is the sole survivor). The enthusiasm and excitement lives on in local 'carnivals'. Performed in the Great Hall of the big house, or out in the tree-studded park, they provided members of the family or household with opportunites for displaying their amateur talents, while songs and dances requiring technical skill would be rendered by professionals.

As they developed (from the time of Henry VIII to that of Charles I) literary composition, orchestral accompaniment and elaborate scenery were added. They reached their zenith in the reign of that extravagant monarch James I. Ben Jonson was writing dialogue, Henry Lawes was supplying the music and Inigo Jones creating the scenery. Expense was no object. Ingenious engines produced astounding effects, colourful costumes dazzled the eye, and lords and ladies danced in slow 'measures' or sprightly 'galliards', manoeuvring behind their masks or disguises. Some appeared as powerful gods and goddesses or as mischievous nymphs and satyrs, but usually they were content to act chorus parts. Scenes quickly succeeded each other, fountains played, fireworks spluttered, trumpets sounded, banners waved – all got up for a one-day wonder.

The subject of a masque was usually allegorical. In one of Jonson's in praise of virtue, Comus, god of cheer, appeared. A 'pastoral' play by John Fletcher (1579–1625), *The Faithful Shepherdess*, may have provided Milton with ideas, such as the herb Moly and the river spirit. *Comus*, possibly performed in the open air and certainly breathing of the English landscape, was produced when the masque was already swiftly going out of fashion through political tension, financial stringency and puritan pressure. The Pastoral, however, had a long literary tradition, going back to Theocritus and Virgil. Originating in an urban longing for a return to rural simplicity, it became a conventional medium for putting across idealist philosophies and romantic sentiments. The imaginary setting was called Arcadian after Arcadia, a mountainous part of central Greece where the shepherd population worshipped Pan.

The occasion for *Comus* was the arrival at Ludlow Castle in 1634 of the Earl of Bridgewater, the new Lord President of the (Welsh) Marches. His children played the principal parts: Lady Alice Egerton, aged fourteen, and her two brothers, John, Viscount Brackley, twelve, and Lord Thomas Egerton, ten. The music was composed by Henry Lawes, a court musician and at the time music master to the children. He asked his friend Milton to write the book, which proved to consist much more of speech-making than of songs. Lawes himself took the part of the Spirit.

Characterization

The characters of *Comus* are as simple as the plot. They reveal their motives and purposes and, in the case of the Lady and Comus, are given full descriptions by others. Comus is the spirit of revelry by night, when the pleasures of the flesh are uninhibited by any sense of sinning. On the other hand, to the revellers they are the fulfilment of natural instinct and a fitting tribute to Beauty itself. In addition to these arguments, Comus relies on the magic goblet, passed to him by his father Bacchus, to transform his 'herd' of followers, and on his wand, a magic gift from his mother Circe, to prevent them from escaping. His persuasive rhetoric is of course Milton arguing, the same heaping of reason on reason which mark his prose pamphlets and which made of Satan a dominating character in the epic. His eulogy of the riches of nature is a fine pastoral performance. As if anticipating the development later in the century of a taste for classical design set in the environment of an English park, Milton has planted his wayward god, embodiment of enticement, firmly in the local landscape.

Comus's opponent, who avoids confrontation with him, also resorts to pastoral disguise. The Attendant Spirit, by appearing first on the scene and adopting the garb of the family shepherd Thyrsis, who is also familiar with the recesses of the wood, puts the mind of the audience at ease where the safety of the travellers is concerned. No matter how careless the brothers were to lose their sister thus, nor how sinister the deception of the 'honest villager', there is no feeling of imminent danger to the heroine.

Metre

Whereas when Comus catches the sound of virgin footsteps he changes from the wild disordered rhythm of his octosyllabic couplets to blank verse speeches of subtle persuasion, the Spirit, who has adopted the truly rural habit of dwelling at length on all related details, in picturesque pastoral pentameters, changes to octosyllabics with fluctuating rhythm, now iambic, now trochaic. Resuming his sky-robes to return to the elements, released like Prospero's Ariel from his mission, he invites those who would follow him into the happy languishment whither he is bound, to love Virtue while still on earth.

Milton called this work simply 'A mask'. It was first printed by Lawes, who had often been asked for copies, and then by the poet himself in 1645, together with other early poems. The next century conferred the title of *Comus* on it: to Milton this might have seemed rather like substituting 'The Triumph of Satan' for *Paradise Lost*. A year before he had contributed on a much smaller scale to *Arcades* an open-air performance connected with the same family. The 'goddess bright' was the Countess of Derby, seventy years old, and with only another year to live. Born Alice Spencer of Althorp, she married to Stanley, the Earl of Derby. Widowed, and retaining her title of Dowager Countess, she married Lord Chancellor Egerton, who was created Viscount Brackley. Lord Brackley's second son, created Earl of Bridgewater, was the Lord President for whom *Comus* was performed away to the north-west. Both pieces would have been written at home, in Horton, some fifteen miles south of Harefield.

Sources for *Comus* have been discovered in several places – but we do well to remember that Milton was still only twenty-five years old. The most acceptable theory is the story that was recorded of the three children having actually been lost in the Hay Wood, south of Ludlow, on their way to the castle.

Summaries and textual notes

Comus (OUP 35)

For more convenient reference, the text is here divided into six sections.

Section 1, lines 1–92

Prologue A Spirit normally attendant on Jupiter announces the errand which has brought him down from the bright celestial world to an overcrowded earth where, with few exceptions, little attention is paid to Virtue. The children of a noble lord (the Earl of Bridgewater) are making their way through a thick wood to the ceremony of installation of their father as Lord President of Wales; he has been sent by Jupiter to protect them.

The wood happens to be the haunt of Comus, god of revelry, who combines the intoxicating power of wine fostered by his father Bacchus, with the magical arts of his mother Circe. To perform his task, the Spirit exchanges his bright robes for the garb of a shepherd in the service of the lord.

discovers Reveals.

Jove's court Jupiter (Jove is a case form) and many of his fellow gods lived according to the ancient Greeks on the lofty summit of Mount Olympus in Thessaly.

mansion i.e. dwelling place, in attendance in the outer court.

insphered i.e. on a plane of their own.

serene Cloudless. The two epithets contrasted with 'the smoke and stir' of the next line.

low-thoughted care i.e. concern solely for their physical condition.

pester'd Obstructed (from higher activity). Originally 'hobbled' like a horse grazing.

pinfold Pound (a small walled-in space) for keeping stray animals till claimed.

Virtue Synonymous in this work with Chastity.

mortal change i.e. from this life to an after life.

ambrosial weeds God-like garments. 'Ambrosia' (not mortal) was the Greek word for the food of the gods.

sin-worn mould Earth worn thin by excess of sin. Milton would have welcomed the modern use of 'eroded'.

by lot Cast by the three sons of Saturn after they had overthrown their father: Jupiter got the land, Neptune the sea, and Pluto (Jupiter of the *nether* regions) the underworld.

unadornèd i.e. otherwise bare – the unbroken surface of the sea.

grace Favour.

By course i.e. each in turn.

several government Individual rule.

tridents Neptune's sceptre was a three-pronged fish-spear. It used to represent the sea-power of Britannia ('this isle').

the main The ocean. Shortened from 'main sea'.

quarters Allots as quarters, or quarters among its four races.

blue-hair'd deities Sea-gods, i.e. rulers of a maritime nation.

fronts the falling sun Faces west.

mickle trust and power Great responsibility and authority.

temper'd awe Strict justice modified by mercy.

old and haughty nation Wales.

new-entrusted sceptre i.e. his installation as Lord president. He held office 1630–1634 and was universally respected.

perplex'd Intricate.

The nodding horror of whose shady brows This line personifies the wood as presenting a scowling face, overshadowed by black locks of hair to the traveller about to enter it. 'Horror' depicts the shaggy edges of the foliage waving up and down (cf. line 88).

Bacchus See section on *The classical element*, beginning on p.12.

misused i.e. taken in excess.

the Tuscan mariners transform'd The Etruscan sailors who once abducted him were turned into dolphins.

Tyrrhene shore The coast of Etruria (roughly the same territory as the later Duchy of Tuscany in central Italy).

Circe's island Aeaea, off the west coast of Italy. Circe was a sorceress whose best known victims were some of Ulysses' sailors.

the Celtic and Iberian fields i.e. France and Spain, where vineyards now flourish.

orient Sparkling (from the sun in the east).

the drouth of Phoebus The parched thirst of one exposed to the hot sun.

ounce Lynx.

All other parts i.e. all except the face. A variation by Milton, from the whole body (see the stage direction following (line 92).

perfect Absolute.

misery Wretched state.

advent'rous Hazardous.

Iris' woof The rainbow, of which Iris was the goddess.

smooth-dittied Filled with melodious words.

nor of less faith And of equal loyalty.

Section 2, lines 93–330

Comus enters with his band – their heads changed into those of animals – dancing and brandishing torches. His song welcomes the approach of night, when sober behaviour and strict discipline can be cast off for intoxicated revelry. Under the moon all nature and the spirits of the wild rejoice, and the devotees of love are ardent to perform their secret rites to the full before open daylight returns. The anti-masque is stopped and the revellers dismissed by Comus when he learns by his art of the approach of a young lady. Intent on adding her to his following, he casts into the air some magic dust which gives him the appearance of a local farm worker.

The Lady, having lost her way and hearing the not too reassuring sound of rustic fun and games, is drawn there to enquire which path to take. She explains aloud that her two brothers have somehow been separated from her in the growing dusk, and now the stars are blotted out.

Puzzled to find no one where she had heard the noise, she calls to mind the good spirits that protect the virtuous, especially the spirit of Chastity. As she expresses her confidence that an angel will be sent if danger threatens, the moon shines out from behind a cloud; to summon her brothers she sings a song to Echo.

The Enchanter is enchanted by the song; comparing it with the voices of the sirens he finds it innocent of hypnotic spell, infused rather with the happiness that wells from a pure heart. He comes forward and addresses her in conventionally flattering terms (quite unsuited to the occupation he seems to follow). Extracting from her (line by line) the reason for her separation from her escorts, he declares he has seen two such young men, but at a great distance. Knowing the wood as well as he does, he will find them by morning, but meanwhile he offers her the shelter of his 'cottage'; she, trusting in the honesty of a humble peasant, accepts.

star Called Hesperus in the evening.

fold Fold his sheep.

the gilded car of day The gilt chariot of Apollo, the sun-god.

His glowing axle Its heated axle.

steep Atlantic stream In classical belief the world was surrounded by a deep river (the Oceanus), part of which washed the coast of North Africa at the foot of the Atlas Mountains. Lines 93–101 are a poetical periphrasis (roundabout phrase) for 'the sun is setting'.

dusky Pole The darkening heavens.

goal Destination.

Rigour Strict discipline.

scrupulous head Conscientious mind (in every detail).

Imitate the starry quire i.e. shine at night.

round A dance in a ring.

finny drove Shoal of fish (moving together). A 'drove' of cattle used to be driven along the roads.

wavering morrice Undulations which suggest the lively movements of morris-dancers.

shelves Rocky ledges.

pert Contemporary synonym of 'dapper'.

fountain brim Edge of a spring.

wakes This word developed from 'watching over the dead' to 'festivals'.

wakes, and wakens These two forms (strong and weak) of the same root must have the same meaning; wakes up of comes to life. Possibly linked with 'wakes' of line 121, especially in view of the line which follows.

makes i.e. exposes as.

Cotytto After addressing his followers, Comus invokes the goddess of debauchery by night, worshipped in various parts of ancient Greece.

Stygian darkness Darkness of Hell, of which the Styx was one of the four rivers.

spets Spits forth.

one blot i.e. complete blackness.

ebon chair Ebony chariot.

Hecat Hecate (see *Diana* in section on *The classical element*).

nice Morn Fastidious Aurora, forerunner of the rising sun.

cabin'd loop-hole The confinement of a narrow slit on the crest of the lofty Himalayas, the farthest known eastern horizon.

descry Announce.

solemnity Festival.

round Cf. line 114.

The Measure Normally a stately dance.

brakes Bushes.

Benighted Caught by the dark.

trains Snares.

as fair a herd i.e. as fine a bunch of dehumanized beings.

dazzling spells i.e. the magic dust that will make him appear as a local inhabitant (cf. line 166).

course Method.

glozing Flattery.

not unplausible i.e. very plausible, seemingly reasonable.

virtue Power

keeps up i.e. he is out late.

gear Affairs, probably sheep.

fairly Gently.

My best guide Since visibility is practically nil.

ill-managed Riotous.

jocund Sprightly.

loose unletter'd hinds Dissolute and ignorant farm workers.

granges Barns.

Pan See section on *The Classical element*.

amiss Wrongly, i.e. irreverently.

wassailers Revellers. From 'wassail' (Old English 'waes hael' be healthy) once used when drinking someone's health.

inform my unacquainted feet Learn which way to take.

blind Obscure, cf. 'blind alley', an occupation which leads nowhere.

spreading favour Kindly spread-out foliage.

a sad votarist in palmer's weed One who has taken a solemn vow to go on pilgrimage and later assumed the garb of a 'palmer' returning from the Holy land.

Rose from the hindmost wheels of Phoebus' wain Followed close on sunset; ('wain': chariot).

the labour of my thoughts Troubling my mind.

single Another way of saying 'nought but'.

airy tongues i.e. the voices of invisible speakers.

syllable Utter distinctly (obsol. as a verb).

men's names Often with fatal results to the men concerned.

astound Terrify.

girt with Hardly appropriate for wings (detachable?).

visibly i.e. with my own eyes, or clearly.

slavish officers Ready instruments.

her silver lining The Latin for cloud (*nubes*) is feminine.

tufted grove Clustered trees.

new enliven'd Reanimated.

Echo See section on *The classical element*.

airy shell Hollow sphere of sound, located like any ordinary shell on the mossy bank of a river (cf. line 276).

slow Meander's margent green The grassy (mossy) bank of the excessively winding Maeander, a river in Asia Minor (from which comes 'meander'); 'margent' archaic for margin.

are The rhyme indicates the contemporary pronunciation.

Parley Two-sided discussion; here, answering back.

daughter of the sphere Just a compliment to one having a connection with music. See the wish expressed in the next line.

give resounding grace Add fresh beauty by echoing (the harmonies).

Earth's mould Cf. line 17.

vocal air The extent of the surrounding air in which the voice is audible.

testify his hidden residence Bear witness that it is there unseen.

fall Cadence.

raven down Softer black plumage in the character of a bird of night: the sinister darkness is coaxed into a good temper (cf. the similar transformation in lines 257–9).

Sirens three Sea nymphs living on a small island off the coast of Sicily who lured sailors by their sweet singing to death on the rocks.

flowery-kirtled Naiades River nymphs in tunics adorned with flowers.

lap it in Elysium Fondle it in paradise.

Scylla See section on *The classical element*.

fell Charybdis Cruel Charybdis. See section on *The classical element*.

attention i.e. to the music. The dogs were silent, while the whirlpool's roar became a murmur.

they i.e. the Sirens and his mother.

robb'd it of itself i.e. made the senses insensible.

sober certainty of waking bliss i.e. undrugged state of conscious happiness.

foreign wonder Wondrous stranger.

rough shades Shady forests.

Unless Unless you are.

Silvan A rustic deity whose worship was limited to Italy; he was half goat, like the satyrs.

blest Endowed with curative powers.

gentle shepherd i.e. Comus in disguise.

extreme shift A last resource.

sever'd company Escort separated from me.

compell'd Drove.

bereft Robbed.

leavy labyrinth Maze with its thick foliage.

near-ushering i.e. who would keep just in front of you.

forestalling Intercepting.

hit Guess at.

Imports their loss i.e. are they only guides?

Hebe's i.e. the lips of Hebe, goddess of youth and for a time cup-bearer to the gods.

labour'd Tired.

In his loose traces i.e. no longer pulling the plough.

swink'd Wearied.

mantling Providing a wide cover.

port Bearing.

element Air.

plighted Plaited, interwoven.

like the path to Heaven i.e. a long way.

it rises i.e. as if to Heaven.

land-pilot's art Navigation by land (coined by Milton).

the sure guess of well-practised feet i.e. the confident steps of one accustomed to using a particular route.

bosky bourn Shrub-lined stream.

from side to side From one end to the other.

ancient neighbourhood i.e. lifelong haunt.

stray attendance your wandering brothers.

shroud Are sheltering.

Ere morrow wake Before the morning comes.

low-roosted i.e. with its nest on the ground.

thatch'd pallet i.e. nest of woven grass.

rouse Rouse itself.

yet is most pretended Is still professed most loudly.

warranted Safe.

Eye me Watch over me.

square my trial ... strength Adjust the severity of my trial to my strength made proportionate to it (repetition of meaning).

Section 3, lines 331–489

Meanwhile the two brothers are lost in another part of the wood unlit by the moon. The elder appeals for light, if not from the sky, then from the window of some humble cot. The younger yearns for sounds of some rural habitation. When he pictures his sister suffering from exposure or at the hands of rough men, the other counsels him against imagining evil before it actually happens. He sees her undismayed, walking in the light of her own virtue. In a philosophical digression he portrays the wise man enjoying the fullness of light in the midst of darkness (to which, indeed, he may have retired), while the wicked man is enclosed in darkness at the height of noon. The more practically-minded younger brother contrasts the security surrounding a poor hermit with the risk run by feminine beauty in such solitude; he fears an attempt on their sister.

While not claiming that she is completely safe, the elder prefers to be optimistic; besides, she has a 'hidden strength'. Questioned about this special protection, he declares it to be Chastity, which enables a woman to travel safely through the wildest and most deserted territory. There is no kind of evil that can really harm Virginity; it endows its possessor with the power to defeat (like Diana), or petrify (like Minerva) any attacker. The chaste Christian is attended by an angelic host whose company imparts a heavenly radiance. On the other hand, impurity defiles and binds the soul to the body it is reluctant to leave.

No sooner has the younger brother conceded his admiration for this dissertation, as pleasing as a musical performance, than they hear the hallo of the Spirit. Not knowing whether it be friend or foe, they draw and wait.

wont'st Art accustomed to.
disinherit Drive out.
Chaos In Greek mythology the primeval shapelessness of the universe.
shades i.e. shadows under trees.
influence i.e. light.
gentle taper A weaker light in comparison with full moonlight.
rush candle The peeled stem of a rush dipped in tallow.
wicker hole This refers to a hut made of wickerwork and clay daub, the window being merely a hole in the structure. The two epithets are distributed one to each noun.
thy long levell'd rule i.e. the taper's horizontal beam.
star of Arcady The Greek pole-star, Arcturus. (See *The classical element* section.)
Tyrian Cynosure The pole star of the Phoenician sailors from Tyre

was in the Lesser Bear, or Cynosura (dog's tail). (See also *The classical element*.)

wattled cotes Sheepfolds with hurdles made of wattle (stakes interlaced with twigs).

pastoral reed with oaten stops A shepherd's pipe with oaten stems. Stops (like 'wicker hole' above) are not strictly 'oaten'.

whistle from the lodge Calling a dog?

close dungeon Locked prison.

innumerous Innumerable.

betake her Resort.

burs Usually spelt 'burrs', prickly seed-heads.

Leans The subject is 'head'.

fraught Burdened.

heat Lust (of some savage).

over-exquisite Too inventive.

date of grief The evil day.

to seek Lacking.

unprincipled Uninstructed in the principles.

bosoms ever Always cherishes in its heart.

single i.e. uncomplicated by any risk.

stir the constant mood of her calm thoughts Upset the steadfast calm of her thoughts. See note on 'wicker hole'.

misbecoming plight A state of distress quite out of character.

seeks to Resorts to.

nurse Wisdom has suffered injury (cf. line 380).

resort Places where crowds gather.

all-to Thoroughly.

sit i' the centre i.e. relax, either amongst the bustling crowd, or at the heart of complete darkness.

walks i.e. he is either lost or restless (having a prison for a mind).

Hesperian tree Guarded in their garden by the three Hesperides, because it bore the three golden apples, a wedding present from Juno to Jupiter. In another version a dragon guarded the tree until killed by Hercules. (Cf. line 982.)

had need Would need.

unenchanted Not subject to any spell (one of the easier ways of overcoming a dragon).

unsunn'd i.e. hitherto hidden away.

wink on Shut its eyes to, pretended not to see.

it recks me not I care not.

dog them both Are closely associated with both (darkness and solitude).

unowned Unrecognized (because out of sight).

poise Balance.

arbitrate th' event Adjudge the (likely) result.

squint suspicion The attitude of mind which cannot see straight and expect the worst.

quiver'd Equipped with a bow and a quiverful of arrows (like a follower of Diana).

trace Traverse.

unharbour'd Without shelter (no cover or protection from wind.)

shagg'd with horrid shades Darkly overgrown with tangled vegetation.

unblench'd Not made to turn pale.

Blue meagre hag Bloodless, skinny witch.

swart Dark of skin.

Antiquity from the old schools of Greece Ancient writers who belonged to one or other of the Greek schools of philosophy (though his first two examples are from mythology).

Hence i.e. for this purpose.

Dian See *Diana* in section on *The classical element*.

brinded Tawny.

pard Leopard.

bolt of Cupid Short blunt-headed arrow used by the god of love.

Gorgon shield Minerva was a powerful virgin goddess of wisdom and the arts. On her shield was the head of Medusa, one of the three monstrous Gorgons, with writhing snakes instead of hair. It had been cut off by Perseus, but was still able to turn to stone those who directly beheld the face.

congeal'd stone Petrified stone. Tautology for emphasis, as 'austerity' repeats 'rigid'.

lackey her Attend her (in their 'liveries' as servants).

oft converse Frequent conversation.

th' outward shape, i.e. the body.

soul's essence i.e. of the same substance as the soul.

all i.e. body and soul.

lavish Extravagant.

inward parts i.e. heart and brain.

Imbodies and imbrutes i.e. becomes identical with flesh, and animal flesh at that. Two coinages by Milton.

property Quality.

damp From exposure. The 'shadows' are ghosts, not figures on the wall caused by rising damp.

Oft seen in charnel-vaults One may well ask 'seen by *whom* in charnel-vaults?' These vaults were used as an underground repository for bones dug up in the churchyard.

And link'd itself 'So' must be understood.

carnal sensualty Fleshly desire. Tautology. The normal spelling is 'sensuality'; here, to suit the metre, there are three syllables instead of five.

How charming In the mouth of a younger brother this would probably be spoken ironically; however, here the author is speaking through him.

crabbèd Churlish.

night-founder'd Overwhelmed by the night (from a ship 'foundering').

comes well Is welcome.

Section 4, lines 490–658

The disguised Spirit is quickly 'recognized' (by members of the family who employ him). Questioned about his being out so late, he explains the importance of his errand; on hearing that they have somehow lost contact with their sister, he now knows that she is in serious danger, but poetic licence allows him a lengthy account of what he has heard and seen.

The old myths and legends are not just stories: the wood is the haunt of Comus and his band of dehumanized revellers, whose riotous behaviour at night is regularly audible. This evening the usual uproar was suddenly stilled, and a voice was heard singing exquisitely. Recognizing it as that of their sister, he ran to the place, found her already in conversation with Comus, heard her ask about her brothers, and so came to find them.

The younger brother then upbraids the elder for his unfounded confidence; the latter counters by reaffirming that Virtue never suffers real defeat, however strongly attacked; and evil, finally separated from good, shall perish by devouring itself. However, coming at last to the point, he brandishes his sword in defiance of all the monsters that ever lived, and prepares to rescue his sister by force.

The Spirit, masquerading as the shepherd Thyrsis, warns him of spells stronger than his sword, but also offers him a magic herb – once given him by a shepherd boy and powerful against all enchantment – to use against Comus. 'Thyrsis' stresses the need to smash Comus's glass and break his wand.

iron stakes i.e. drawn swords.

madrigal Originally a pastoral song (from Greek *mandra*, a sheepfold).

pent Folded.

next joy i.e. the younger brother.

the stealth i.e. the stolen sheep.

How chance How does it happen.

sadly In all seriousness.

blame i.e. blameworthy act.

vain or fabulous Untrue or legendary.

storied Narrated.

Chimeras The Chimera was a monster, compounded of lion, goat and dragon, which breathed fire.

unbelief is blind Proverbially, 'None so blind as he who will not see.'

navel Centre.

murmurs Whispered spells.

fixes instead i.e. fastens on in place of the human visage; 'likeness' is the object of the verb.

unmoulding reason's mintage ... face i.e. destroying the inscription (as on a coin) that has been stamped by reason.

brow this bottom glade Rise above this glade at the bottom of the valley.

stabled i.e. that have broken into a shed where domestic animals are kept.

obscurèd haunts of inmost bowers i.e. in out-of-the-way corners where they gather in secret.

unweeting Unwittingly (ignorant of the danger).

savoury herb Tasty herbage.

knot-grass A weed with many branching stems.

dew-besprent Sprinkled with dew (in the evening).

meditate Practise.

ere a close Before I reached the first cadence.

drowsy-frighted Frightened out of their natural drowsiness.

litter More suitable than a chariot for such a god as Somnus, usually represented asleep on a feather bed screened by black curtains. Here the litter may be understood to bring sleep to others.

silence A personification, not a mythological being.

be never more ... displaced Cease to exist if such music could take her place.

create a soul ... Death Breathe life into a dead body.

harrow'd Torn.

in sly disguise i.e. the villager of lines 166 and 576.

period sentence.

erring Wrong-headed.

pillar'd firmament The sky (a solid roof) supported by mountains.

sooty flag Black banner.

Acheron A river of Hell, and so Hell itself.

Harpies Winged monsters with women's faces, the bodies of vultures, and sharp claws, fouling everything they touched.

Hydras The Hydra had a varying number of heads; when one was cut off, two grew in its place, until Hercules used a burning iron to destroy the monster.

his purchase The prize he has seized.

by the curls By Comus's hair. How did the elder brother know that the enchanter took after his father Bacchus in this respect?

yet Nevertheless.

emprise Enterprise, undertaking.

stead Service.

unthread Loosen.

surprisal Being suddenly seized.

simples Single herbs (that could be 'compounded' into medicines).

like esteem'd i.e. unregarded.

clouted shoon Studded shoes (bruising with their tread).

Moly A magic herb given Ulysses by Mercury to protect himself against the magic of Circe, Comus's mother.

Haemony Moly is legendary; Haemony is Milton's invention, possibly from Haemonia, the original name of Thessaly, which had magic associations.

Furies' apparition Appearance of the Furies, the three fierce women who carried out the vengeance of the gods.

little reckoning made i.e. paid little regard to it.

extremity Time of need.

though disguised i.e. Comus, not Thyrsis; 'by this means' seems to contradict line 572 'by certain signs'.

lime-twigs Bird lime on twigs to snare birds. Here the most dangerous area of Comus's spells.

menace high Loud-sounding threats.

sons of Vulcan Vulcan, Roman god of fire and metal-forging, had a number of sons, one of whom, Cacus, a three-headed moster, breathed fire.

Section 5, lines 659–813

The scene changes to Comus's enchanted palace. When he sees the Lady refuse his magic liquor, he threatens her with the paralysing power of his wand. She declares he cannot chain her mind. He goes on to boast of the stimulating effect of the drink and to rebuke her for being so niggardly with her beauteous self. The drink, moreover, will banish her fatigue. She still rejects what can only be the reverse of delicious: one more deception added to those he has already played on her.

Comus next criticizes those who practise abstinence: scorning the abundance and variety of food and drink, rich raiment and jewellery. To renounce these in a fit of temperance, eating no meat, drinking only water, and wearing the coarsest of clothes, would be to treat God as if He were a miserly distributor of His gifts. Thus Nature would be smothered in her own excess. The Lady must not be taken in by the idea of Virginity – beauty is to be traded and enjoyed in common, otherwise it languishes. Beauty is for courtly festivities, whereas the plain may stay at home busied in domestic duties; beauty is a gift with a condition attached.

The Lady, while preferring silence, is roused by such specious arguments to speak up for Virtue. Nature's resources are not superfluous, but could and should be shared more equally among men. This would be the right way to worship, not by greedy, blasphemous behaviour. But why seek to convince an uncomprehending enemy of the spiritual power of Chastity, or set forth the doctrine of Virginity? With all his eloquence, he deserves to remain in blissful ignorance; though should she attempt the task, her words would be so inspired with burning conviction that the whole earth would, in its convulsions of sympathy, bring crashing down upon him all the creations of his magic.

Disturbed by a sense of something stronger than his powers, Comus adopts a more forceful tone and prepares to thrust his pretended curative down her throat.

nerves Sinews.

chain'd up in alabaster Made incapable of movement, as in an alabaster statue.

Daphne See *The classical element.*

corporal rind Outer shape of my body.

cordial julep Invigorating sweet drink, of Persian origin.

bounds i.e. the glass of the goblet.

that Nepenthes ... wife of Thonè ... Helena Nepenthes (an oriental shrub that devours insects) was given by Polydamna, wife of Thonè,

King of Egypt, to Helen ('of Troy'), daughter of Jupiter by Tyndarus's wife Leda. Helen used the nepenthes to drug the drink of her husband Menelaus and his friends.

invert the covenants Follow the opposite of the agreed terms. This is paraphrased in the next two lines.

unexempt From which no one is excused.

That have been tired The antecedent is either 'mortal frailty' line 686, or 'you' line 682 (the Lady has only recently been isolated, but this may refer to their day's journey).

visor'd Wearing a mask. Comus has assumed his normal appearance.

lickerish Temptingly delicious.

draught Drink.

budge doctors Learned men in gowns trimmed with 'budge' fur, the kind indicating the school.

Stoic From the 'stoa' or porch in which taught Zeno, the founder of this philosophy, which was later interpreted as advocating indifference to pain or pleasure.

Cynic tub The famous barrel in which Diogenes, a leading cynic, took to living as a demonstration of disregard for ease, and contempt for conventional pretences. The name is derived from Greek 'kuon', dog.

Abstinence As a means to virtue this was praised by both the Cynics, and by the Stoics who developed from them.

curious Fastidious.

green shops The young mulberry leaves on which the larvae of silkworms feed. The site of Buckingham Palace was laid out by James I as a mulberry garden to encourage the silk industry in Britain.

in her own loins i.e. underground.

hutch'd Stored away (like a treasure in a chest).

pulse The old word for peas and beans, here suggesting a vegetarian diet.

frieze coarse woollen cloth.

Who The antecedent is 'Nature'.

strangled Suffocated.

o'erfraught Overladen.

th' unsought diamonds ... stars i.e. the diamonds left unmined would light up the dark cliff-face of the underworld with a heraldic kind of device, covering it with points of light (like the iron studs on an old door).

with shameless brows Without blinking in a shame-faced way, like one accustomed to the dark.

cozen'd Cheated.

unsavoury in th' enjoyment of itself Lacking savour when refusing to share itself with others.

languish'd Drooping – 'languish' is strictly intransitive.

time Opportunity.

brag Creation to boast about.

sorry grain Poor texture.

ply/The sampler Work at a piece of fancy embroidery.

tease Comb in preparation for spinning.

vermeil-tinctured Rich red in colour.

like the morn fair The fashionable colour in those days.

think to charm ... as mine eyes Think he has cast a spell on my mental powers as he has on my eyesight (by appearing as a villager – see 'garb' in next line).

Obtruding false rules ... garb Thrusting before me immoral principles dressed up in reasonable arguments.

bolt Let fly (as an arrow).

unsuperfluous i.e. with nothing in excess.

due Duly.

blasphemes his Feeder By its behaviour, Gluttony insults the One who provies the food.

sun-clad Strengthened by undimmed brightness.

Fain Gladly.

art worthy ... know Does not deserve to know.

lot i.e. pitiful state.

dear Previous.

fence Word-play (from fencing with a sword).

brute i.e. otherwise unfeeling. Cf. 'dumb things' in line 796.

lend her nerves Bring her sinews to bear.

She fables not She is not making this up.

set off by Supported by.

though not mortal Though I am not mortal.

thunder The characteristic weapon (causing more terror than damage) of Jupiter, Zeus and Thor, reigning gods of Romans, Greeks and Teutons.

the chains of Erebus i.e. imprisonment in Hell (one of its classical names).

Saturn's crew The Titans were twelve in number; brothers and sisters of giant size. Saturn was the youngest; he was defeated by his son Jupiter who imprisoned the giants (not the Titans) in Hell.

dissemble i.e. pretend that he is not impressed.

canon laws of our foundation Treating his 'crew' as if they were a religious order.

'tis but the lees ... blood i.e. her mood is the residue from too much
  black bile, the 'humour' which was believed to cause depression; its
  density led to 'settling' on the bottom of the blood stream.
straight Immediately.

Section 6, lines 814–1023

The brothers, having broken in on Comus's attempt and driven
him and his band away, are followed in by the Spirit, who reminds
them that they should have seized the wand, without which they
cannot release their rescued sister from her immobility. However,
he quickly remembers the nymph Sabrina (with a full account of
how she came to be the goddess of the Severn and of her present
rural avocations), and proposes to appeal to her to help another
virgin in distress. This he does in a song of one stanza, and then an
elaborate invocation.

  Sabrina, accompanied by her nymphs, comes into view and sings
a stanza of greeting. Introduced to the motionless maiden, she
sprinkes precious drops of her river water on fingers and lips, finally
applying the coolness of her palms to the adhesive power holding
the Lady to the enchanted chair. The Spirit follows Sabrina's
departure with a blessing, then offers to guide the three to their
father's castle. At Ludlow, country dances (part of the celebra-
tions) are interrupted by the familiar figure of 'Thyrsis' (where,
one wonders, is the real shepherd?) in order to present the lost
children to their parents after their ordeal in the haunts of Comus.

  Whether he does this as Thyrsis or as the Attendant Spirit, having
discarded his shepherd's smock for his 'sky-robes', only the original
producer, like his successors, can say. In the Epilogue he announces
his return to the celestial spheres where the gods live out their
immortal lives in an ideal landscape bathed by eternal summer. As
he leaves on his journey into space, he recommends his hearers to
love Virtue always and so find their way to (another) Heaven.

without his rod reversed ... power Unless you wave his rod in the
  reverse direction and say his spells backwards to break the hold he has.
Meliboeus A shepherd's name in one of Virgil's 'Eclogues'.
moist curb Liquid power.

Sabrina The name of the River Severn is derived from this illegitimate daughter of Locrine, who reigned after his father Brutus, legendary founder of Britain. She and her mother were drowned in the river by Locrine's jealous queen, Gwendolen.

pearlèd Adorned with pearls.

Nereus Ancient sea-god and father of the fifty sea-nymphs or Nereïds.

lavers Bowls (containing nectar).

asphodel A legendary flower of fields in which the heroic dead reclined after arrival in their part of the underworld.

ambrosial i.e. distilled from the food of the gods.

Helping i.e. curing.

urchin blasts Disease caused by 'urchins' i.e. hedgehogs, once believed to have an evil influence.

viall'd liquors Liquid medicines from phials.

the old swain i.e. Meliboeus.

clasping charm Spell that binds.

amber-dropping i.e. fragrant from ambergris (a perfume).

lake River (now dialect).

Oceanus Eldest of the Titans and predecessor of Neptune as god of the sea, especially the great river encircling the earth in a clockwise direction. Tethys was his wife, another Titan, and Nereus was his son (cf. line 835).

Carpathian wizard's hook The crook of Proteus, another son of Oceanus, who tended Neptune's herds, the seals. He lived on an island in the Carpathian Sea (part of the Eastern Mediterranean). He could change shape instantly, particularly to avoid answering awkward questions.

Triton's winding shell See *The classical element* section.

Glaucus' spell See *The classical element.*

Leucothea Ino, fair-skinned wife of a husband driven mad by another of Juno's intrigues, threw herself and son into the sea; the gods made her a sea divinity names 'leuko-thea', white goddess. Her son became known as Palaemon, god of harbours.

Thetis' tinsel-slipper'd feet The mother of Achilles is described as 'silver-footed' (in Homer). 'Tinsel' refers to any glittering substance.

Parthenope's dear tomb Parthenope was what is now Naples (*Neapolis*: 'new city'). The city's original Greek name of Parthenope was that of a siren found dead on the shore.

fair Ligea One of the three Sirens.

coral-paven bed River-bed paved with coral.

printless Leaving no footmark.

office best Chief duty.

of glutinous heat That are sticky when hot.

Amphitrite's bower The cave of Neptune's wife.

old Anchises' line Anchises was the father of Aeneas, whose grandson Brutus was the father of Locrine (see line 827).

singèd Heated.

tresses Foliage of trees on the banks.

molten crystal i.e. clear water.

beryl A yellow green precious stone. Possibly this, with 'golden ore', is descriptive of the waves, possibly a wish for wealth for the Severn valley.

wish'd presence Express their gratitude for his acceding to their wishes by being present.

Hesperus See lines 393–9.

crispèd Curled; cf. 'shagged', line 429.

The Graces Three daughters of Venus, beautiful virgins who presided over all kind offices. Cf. L'Allegro, 2,1–15.

Hours See p.15

musky Smelling of musk, a perfume.

cedarn alleys Paths among cedars.

Nard and cassia's balmy smells Fragrant scents of two oriental spices.

humid bow i.e. rainbow seen through rain-drops.

blow Are covered with (flowers).

purfled scarf Coloured silk band.

Elysian Heavenly.

be true i.e. are capable of recognizing the truth.

Adonis See *The classical element*.

Assyrian queen Venus, so-called here from her identification by some worshippers with Astarte, the Syrian goddess of love.

Celestial Cupid A change from the 'frivolous' of line 445.

advanced Promoted.

Psyche See *The classical element*.

bow'd welkin Arched sky.

sphery chime i.e. The 'spheres' with their 'music'.

Arcades (OUP 30)

Fragments of verse, monologue and songs, contributed by Milton to a masque at Harefield Place, a large manor house then existing in the village of Harefield, near Uxbridge, Middlesex. (The Dowager Countess of Derby is seated either in the Great Hall or in the park to receive the tributes of members of her large family.)

1 Song

The Arcades, inhabitants of Arcadia, composed of nymphs and shepherds, draw near the object of their search, the grand lady whose fame, previously considered excessive, is now inadequate for such a goddess.

Monologue

The Genius of the Wood offers to guide them (to one at whose presence they have practically arrived), first explaining in much descriptive detail his functions as the 'Power' of the wood, encouraging the vegetation by day, by night enjoying the 'music of the spheres' (inaudible to human ears) which exerts a benign influence on the world below. Such celestial sounds would be the best form of praise to the illustrious lady, but instead he will attempt something in a lower key as he accompanies them to where she sits in state.

2 Song

Across the lawn, beneath the trees, he leads the Arcades to the 'Queen'.

3 Song

After their dance of greeting the Spirit invites them to leave for good the (imaginary) land they have come from, to serve a queen better than anyone by whom Arcadia has hitherto been governed.

descry Catch sight of.
our vows and wishes bend Our prayers and desires are turned.
erst Formerly.
Envy On the part of Fame or of those who only half-praised her?
Latona Mother of Apollo and Diana by Jupiter; (See *The classical*

element). Though persecuted by Juno she became a powerful goddess, and her twins were still more celebrated.

Cybele Wife of Saturn and mother of Jupiter and his brother gods; portrayed with towers on her head. Juno would be her daughter-in-law.

give her odds Treat her as an inferior; 'odds' were an allowance given to a weaker side.

gentle Well-born.

swains Countrymen, especially shepherds. There is a contradiction between the young people's appearance and their speech and carriage.

Arcady The land-locked province of Arcadia in the middle of the Peloponnesus, Southern Greece, named after Arcas, son of Jupiter. It was famous for its oaks and mountains and its people were mostly shepherds, fighters and musicians; Pan lived among them. In Renaissance literature it became an idyllic setting for song, romance and philosophic discussion.

Alpheus An Arcadian river-god who loved a nymph named Arethusa until she was changed into a fountain in Sicily; it was believed that he disappeared underground and under the Mediterranean to rejoin her there.

breathing roses i.e. in human form – the Genius has turned to the nymphs.

silver-buskin'd Wearing half-boots adorned with silver – for use in the woods.

solemnity Festival.

shallow-searching Superficial or grudging.

Curl the grove ... ringlets Give the wood its characteristic leafy appearance.

wanton windings wove Woven with luxuriant intertwined growths.

noisome Damaging.

blasting Blighting.

evil dew Fungus.

thwarting thunder blue Local lightning flashes (harmless).

cross dire-looking planet Malignant star.

tassell'd horn i.e. of the huntsman.

puissant Having a powerful effect.

murmurs Whispered spells.

Sirens' harmony i.e. the music of the spheres, on each of which sat a siren, their combined notes forming a harmony.

infolded Concentric, one within another, with each corresponding in size to a planet's distance from Earth.

those that hold the vital shears The Three Fates, the third cutting the thread of life.

adamantine spindle i.e. the axis of the earth and planets. The original spindle was a simple rod, the twisting of which turned loose fibres into thread. Here it is a huge invisible rod or 'pole', but without any thread. Adamant was a legendary material of infinite hardness (from a Greek word for 'untameable'); it now describes an inflexible attitude.

Necessity Mother of the Fates, who could perhaps be lulled by music into reduced activity.

the low world ... heavenly tune (Lead) the earth in regulated movement in accordance with the music of the spheres.

hand or voice i.e. instrumental of vocal music.

assay Attempt (in the songs that follow).

stem Birth.

enamell'd Glossy.

the warbled string i.e. the instrument that accompanies the singing.

star-proof That keeps out the light of the stars.

Ladon River in Arcadia that joins the Alphaeus.

Lycaeus A mountain in southern Arcadia, but Cyllene is on the west coast of the Peloponnesus. Erymanth is a mountain in northern Arcadia, Maenalus in the south.

your loss deplore Grieve at your departure.

grace Privilege.

Syrinx Daughter of Ladon who requested the gods to change her into a reed rather than yield to Pan. The latter made his pipe out of her reeds.

On the Morning of Christ's Nativity (OUP 1)

Introductory Stanzas

1–2

The Day of the Incarnation and its purpose – to redeem mankind and create peace.

3–4

The poet appeals to his Muse to offer a welcoming ode before the Wise Men reach the manger.

The Hymn

1–4

To a Nature guiltily hiding beneath a mantle of snow, Peace is sent to bring a truce for every conflict.

5–7

Not only was the night peaceful, but stars lingered on beyond their time, while the sun was reluctant to appear, outshone by the Light of the World.

8–12

The simple shepherds are surprised by heavenly harmony announcing a new dominion of the sky and by dazzling light revealing an angelic host chanting in praise of the 'New-born Heir', in song unheard since the days of Creation.

13–15

The poet calls on such celestial music to make itself heard, destroying evil and bringing back Truth and Justice (tempered by Mercy).

16–18

But Fate decrees that first this infant must redeem sinners on the Cross, and the dreaded Last Judgment must take place. However, the timeless process has begun; and Evil, the dragon, fears diminution of his powers.

19–21

Apollo is silent in his temple; the vanished Geniuses of nature are mourned by nymphs of streams and woods; the dying moans of household gods terrify their priests.

22–24

Nearer the birthplace of the infant the Syrian gods and goddesses and the strange animal deities of Egypt are driven out, abandoning their worshippers.

25–27

The Babe, with the supernatural strength of an infant Hercules, deals not only with Osiris, but also with the monster Typhon. At sunrise on this natal day all heathen powers shrink back into the Underworld, all ghosts return to their graves, and the local spirits surviving in contemporary superstition disappear with the darkness. The song ends with the Christ child asleep in the stable.

Introduction

our deadly forfeit should release Would remit the penalty of death brought on mankind by Adam's disobedience.

work us Create for us.

Trinal Unity i.e. the Trinity of Father, Son and Holy Spirit.

Muse Invoked by poets and usually not named. Of the nine Muses, concerned with poetry and of the arts, Euterpe inspired lyric poetry.

sacred vein Divine inspiration.

Afford Offer.

spangled host i.e. the stars, whose points of light glitter like 'spangles' of tinsel.

star-led Wizards The Three Wise Men who were led by a moving star to the birthplace in Bethlehem.

odours Frankincense.

prevent them Get there before them.

touch'd with hallow'd fire Inspired with holy zeal, describing the voice; for 'fire' see Isaiah 6,6–7.

The Hymn

1–12

meanly Shabbily (Joseph was not necessarily poor).

rude Roughly made, i.e. when used as a cradle.

gaudy trim Colourful adornment, i.e. blossoms (it was wintertime).

woos A change to 'historic present', making the past more immediate. Particularly effective later in the flight of the pagan gods.

guilty front Expression of guilt (on her face). The guilt is human.

naked shame The shame of her nakedness (leafless state).

Pollute with sinful blame Stained with the marks of sins deserving of blame.

saintly veil Metaphor for the literal snow of 1,39.

her Maker's eyes i.e. the eyes of the Holy Infant, but identical with those of God the Creator.

foul deformities Probably the destruction wrought by wars.

olive green The goddess of Peace was usually represented with an olive branch in her hand.

the turning sphere Either the whole system of transparent, revolving concentric spheres with the earth as centre, in each of which a planet was embedded, or the particular sphere of Venus (Love), with whom Peace seems to be temporarily identified in 1,50.

harbinger Originally an officer sent in advance of an army to obtain accommodation, hence generally a forerunner. Here of God Himself, about to be born in human form.

turtle wing i.e. the wings of doves ('turtle-doves'), which drew the chariot of Venus. These, together with the 'amorous' clouds and the myrtle wand, must refer to the goddess of love.

strikes Not a very harmonious word for spreading peace.

hookèd With scythes on its wheels to cut down an enemy.

awful Filled with awe.

sovran Supreme. The same as 'sovereign'.

whist Hushed. Hence the gentleness of the next line.

birds of calm Halcyons. (See *The classical element*).

one way i.e. in the direction of Bethlehem.

influence The power believed then (and since) to be exerted by stars on human fortunes.

Lucifer The planet Venus when preceding sunrise. The name 'light-bringer' was wrongly applied to Satan.

orbs Spheres of 'influence'.

bespake Gave orders.

As As if.

inferior flame Brightness less than that of the Child.

new-enlight'ned Just being illuminated by a new light.

burning axle-tree The axle of the sun's chariot, heated by the sun's temperature or by the speed of travel.

lawn Field of pasture.

the point of dawn Cf. French 'point du jour'.

than Then.

Pan Personification of nature as well as god of shepherds.

kindly Out of the kindness of his heart or in *kinship* with humanity (or both).

strook Struck out.

Answering the stringèd noise Keeping in tune with the sound of stringed instruments.

close Cadence.

Cynthia's seat The moon. Cynthia was another name for Diana. The moon is no longer regarded as a 'hollow' sphere.

the airy region thrilling Piercing the upper air. The original meaning of 'thrill'.

happier i.e. happier than when Heaven and Nature were independent.

the shame-faced night array'd Put to flight the bashful night. The original word was 'shamefast'.

Cherubim ... Seraphim In the Old Testament, the two chief orders in the hierarchy of celestial beings attendant upon God.

unexpressive Beyond human expression.

the Sons of Morning Possibly suggested by Job 38,7.

the well-balanced world ... hung Hung the world on 'hinges' (a derivation of 'hang'), so that it turned smoothly. A reference to the polar axis. In *Paradise Regained* , 4,415 Milton uses 'four hinges' for the cardinal points.

cast Dug out.

weltering Wildly tossing.

13–21

ninefold harmony Music of the nine spheres.

consort Musical accompaniment (by confusion with 'concert').

symphony Voices in harmony.

long The angels' song did not indeed last long!

Time will run back The future simple corresponds to the historic present of this passage (see stanza 16).

speckled Vanity Human worthlessness covered in blemishes.

earthly mould i.e. human bodies.

to the peering day For day to peep cautiously into.

Orb'd Encircled (strictly, half a circle).

like glories wearing Appearing in similar splendour.

in celestial sheen In bright heavenly garments.

redeem our loss Buy back what was lost by Adam's sin.

ychain'd in sleep i.e. the dead. Archaic prefix.

wakeful trump of doom i.e. the trumpet announcing the Last Judgement and rousing the dead.

Mount Sinai For the eruption and the trumpet, see Exodus, 19,16–19.

session Legal term for what is an assembly of humanity at the Day of Judgement.

dreadful Inspiring dread (and contrasting with 'bliss' below).

middle air A space between earth (from which the dead will arise), and heaven (to which, if deserving, they will ascend).

But now begins Returning to the Nativity and the panorama of disappearing heathen powers.

old Dragon See Revelation 12,9, and 20,2–3.

straiter Narrower.

Swinges Flourishes (in a threatening manner).

folded Coiled.

hideous Terrifying.

archèd roof Of the temple erected near the site of the oracle.

in words deceiving i.e. the ambiguous prophetic utterances by the priest serving the oracle.

Apollo The god of poetry among other things, whose oracles were consulted at various temples, the chief being at Delphi. (See also *The classical element.*)

cell Inner sanctum.

loud lament Second object of 'heard'.

haunted Each natural feature, e.g. wood, stream or hill, had its own guardian spirit, as well as attendant nymphs.

consecrated earth Sacred plot used for offerings to the Lemures, spirits of the dead.

holy hearth Where the Lares, gods of the household, were represented by effigies, to which incense was burnt.

Flamens Roman priests, each dedicated to the service of a particular god.

quaint Elaborate.

the chill marble seems to swear A bad omen.

peculiar power Individual god.

22–27

Peor and Baälim The Phoenicians worshipped various forms of Baäl (a Semitic word meaning 'god of the place', i.e. a local god. Baälim is the plural form. Baäl-peor (see Deuteronomy 4,3) was the local god of Peor.

god of Palestine Dagon was twice thrown down when the captured

Ark of the Hebrews was placed by the Philistines in his temple (see 1 Samuel, 5,1–7).

Ashtaroth The Canaanites' and Phoenicians' goddess of fertility and of love (The Greek Astarte).

mother i.e. of the other gods of Phoenicia.

Lybic Hammon The temple of Jupiter-Ammon (who had ram's horns) was in an oasis in the Libyan desert. He was a blend of the Roman god with the Egyptian Amun or Amen.

shrinks Draws in (with fear).

Thammuz A handsome youth beloved of Ashtaroth, but killed by a boar. The story may be the original of that of Venus and Adonis (another form of Thammuz). Tyre was a Phoenician town. (See Ezekiel, 8,14).

Moloch God of the Ammonites, a race east of the Jordan, whose capital was approximately where Amman is now. Children were sacrificed to Moloch by being thrown into the arms of his 'burning idol'.

blackest hue i.e. the darkness of Hell.

brutish i.e. in the shape of animals, or having animals' heads.

Isis ... Orus ... Anubis Egyptian gods.

Osiris This important Egyptian god was represented, in living form as a sacred bull, at his temple at Memphis.

unshower'd Unfed by rain.

shroud Refuge.

timbrell'd anthems Chants accompanied by 'timbrels' (tambourines).

sable-stolèd sorcerers Magicians wearing black stoles (priestly scarves).

ark The sacred Egyptian chest of line 217. The Hebrew Ark contained tables of the Law.

He feels i.e. Osiris feels.

hand Power. This seems incompatible with a cradle, but the answer is in line 228.

rays of Bethlehem i.e. light from the manger.

dusky eyne Dark eyes (Egyptian); the archaic 'eyne' fits the rhyme.

beside Besides Osiris.

Typhon Regarded by the Egyptians as the source of all evil and represented as a wolf or crocodile.

swaddling·bands These were an infant's first clothes, in the form of bandages.

crew Band.

orient Eastern. The direction of sunrise (if that is what is being depicted!)

infernal jail The prison in Hell whither ghosts had to return by sunrise.

fetter'd ghost Spirit chained to his sinful past. Cf. *Comus*, 473 and Marley's ghost in Dicken's *A Christmas Carol*.

several Individual.

yellow-skirted fays Fairies whose dresses, as they fly away into the receding night, are caught by the first rays of the rising sun. ('Fay' from 'fée', French for 'fairy'.)

night-steeds Horses drawing the chariot of the goddess Night (strictly owls or bats).

moon-loved maze Intricate dance which they love to perform in the light of the moon, winding in and out of the tree trunks.

youngest-teemèd star Latest born star which was followed by the Wise Men).

fix'd her polish'd car Halted her chariot.

courtly stable i.e. transformed by the presence of God and His angels.

serviceable Ready to serve.

Lycidas

Background to the poem

Edward King was drowned in the Irish Sea in August 1637, at the age of twenty-five. He was younger than Milton, but already a Fellow of their old college, Christ's at Cambridge; and he promised well in his chosen vocation of priest. His friends invited Milton to join in a tribute (published in 1638). While not a very close friend, the poet readily responded with one of the greatest elegies in our language.

In a pastoral elegy the conventional fiction of shepherds and their flocks is a degree removed from the direct expression of personal sorrow, but it provides the framework for rich poetical imagination, musical utterance and the usual colourful legendary links with primeval nature. That Milton was certainly moved by deep sympathy is shown by his open declaration that this was one more composition (the last probably being *Comus*, three years before) undertaken reluctantly but out of a sense of duty while he still considered himself unready to write poetry that would endure.

Powerful feelings rarely produce literary works of art, as is shown in the invective with which Milton assails the priests or college ordinands he has observed. This startling digression (important enough in his eyes to be mentioned in the sub-title) is a foretaste of the prose polemics he was to launch in the near future – no longer verdant woods and pastures but the corridors of power, and a scaffold for a king in Whitehall.

Summary

The poet has turned to verse again, though his poetic faculty is still not fully developed. The occasion is a sad one, a tribute to a fellow poet lost at sea in the flower of his youth.

He calls on the Muses (who may one day mourn his own passing) to help him lament the shepherd with whom he has been so closely associated in daily pastoral duties. They have together composed songs to the flute, with the woodland spirits listening to their echoes. Now the shepherd is gone his loss is felt as severely as would the blight of some deadly disease, or a late frost.

No sooner does the poet ask why the nymphs of North Wales had not been there to rescue his friend than he realizes the futility of the question. The Muses could not save Orpheus from the frenzied rage of the Bacchae. He goes on to ask why, in such a cruel world, a shepherd should labour over his verses instead of enjoying himself in the company of the nymphs. Fame is a stimulus to hard work, but what if death intervenes? This query is answered by no less a person than Apollo: praise, unlike mankind, is not mortal. True fame does not grow out of the chatter of worldly critics, but is awarded to the deserving by Jove in Heaven.

Now the poet records the testimony of the sea deities that no storm of theirs had drowned Lycidas; the ship had been badly built, or built under a curse.

Camus (the river Cam: Cambridge University) bewails the loss of his loved son. The Pilot (St Peter, here representing the Church of England) in a bitter harangue exclaims that he would have exchanged for Lycidas any of the unworthy pastors of neglected flocks; these are more concerned with personal promotion than with the spiritual welfare of their congregations – who are fobbed off with unedifying sermons or false doctrines.

Let all the springs and meadows of Arcadia bring their tribute of flowers and tears to heap on the dead shepherd's bier, wherever that may be: tossed in the wild ocean beyond the Hebrides or reclining beneath the walls of St Michael's Mount. He appeals to St Michael himself to search the home waters for Lycidas, and to the dolphins to bring him ashore.

The bereaved shepherds must cease to weep for one who, like a revolving star, though drowned in the sea, has now ascended through the risen Christ to the sky, where the union of Joy with Love is celebrated in song by the heavenly host. He also addresses Lycidas as the new local Genius of the Irish Sea.

The shepherd himself is given an envoi as, having piped all day, he rises to his feet, prepared to look upon a different landscape the next day.

Lycidas A shepherd's name from one of Virgil's 'Eclogues'.

Monody A lament or dirge, solo instead of a chorus.

by occasion Incidentally.

yet once more This emphatic opening phrase expresses unwillingness to resume poetic composition, as he feels his style is still unripe.

laurels With myrtle and ivy, to make a poet's garland for the dead man.

the mellowing year The use of 'year' instead of 'season' indicates the poet is thinking of the future year in which at last his technique is perfected. Meanwhile the hand compelled by sad circumstance to pluck the berries is still unskilled.

constraint Compulsion.

disturb your season due Prevent your ripening in due course.

knew Was able.

welter to the parching wind Be tossed about by the withering wind.

meed Tribute.

Sisters The Nine Muses, whose sacred fountain on Mount Helicon flowed from under the altar to Jove. Poets often invoked them for inspiration.

somewhat loudly i.e. in passionate mourning.

Muse i.e. inspired poet.

With lucky words ... urn Utter the same kind words to wish me well over my ashes at some future date.

sable shroud Dark shelter (the modern meaning would be incompatible with ashes in an urn).

the high lawns appear'd The grass-vcovered hills became visible.

heard Listened.

gray-fly Otherwise known as the trumpet-fly.

winds her sultry horn Hums in the heat of the day.

the star The planet Venus, in those days called Hesperus in the evening, Lucifer in the morning.

Temper'd to the oaten flute Modulated to the sound of flutes made of oaten straw instead of reeds.

Satyrs ... Fauns The Greek and Latin words for rural creatures with hairy bodies, goats' legs and short horns on their heads, given to the pursuit of nymphs.

Damoetas Probably a tutor at Christ's College is intended.

desert Empty.

gadding vine Any wild climbing plant (e.g. Traveller's Joy).

taint-worm Cattle disease.

weanling i.e. (cattle) that have been weaned – no longer suckling.

wardrop Wardrobe, here meaning blossoms.

the white-thorn blows The hawthorn comes into bloom (a time of late frosts).

Mona Anglesey to the English. Its woods were once a Druid centre until it was destroyed by the Romans. 'Shaggy' describes the trees, but the 'top of Mona high' is the error of one who has never visited the island.

wizard stream The Deva (River Dee) changed its course frequently and had magic associations. It flowed into the Irish Sea, where the ship carrying Lycidas foundered.

Orpheus After losing Eurydice he was inconsolable and so offended the women of Thrace that in a Bacchanalian 'rout' they tore him to pieces and threw his head into the River Hebrus (the Marissa), which flows into the Aegean Sea some sixty miles north of the island of Lesbos (Mitylene).

thankless Muse Poetry gets scant rewards.

Amaryllis ... Neaera Shepherdesses' names in classical pastoral poetry.

last infirmity i.e. the weakness (love of fame) which overtakes it in the end.

guerdon Reward. (Object of 'find'.)

blind Fury Strictly, the third of the three Fates: Clotho spinning the thread of our individual lives, Lachesis measuring the fated length, and Atropos cutting it. The three Furies were tormenting spirits who persecuted the guilty in this life and the next. Milton's added epithet suggests that death strikes blindly.

Phoebus A name ('Bright One') of Apollo. (See *The classical element.*)

glistering foil Shining metallic sheet (of no value in itself).

broad rumour General reputation.

Arethuse (Usually 'Arethusa'); a nymph pursued by the river-god
Alphaeus. (See section on *The classical element.*)

Mincius A river in northern Italy, near which Virgil was born (hence
'honoured').

That strain i.e. the utterance of Phoebus.

my oat My pipe (which – strictly – plays, not hears). The singer repeats
what he has heard.

Herald of the Sea Probably Triton, son of Neptune, half man, half
dolphin, and his father's messenger.

in Neptune's plea Acting as defence against the charge of drowning
Lycidas.

felon i.e. treacherous.

gust of rugged wings Rough blast.

beakèd Sharp-pointed.

not of his story Nothing about the allegation he was investigating.

Hippotades Aeolus (son of Hippotas) was given charge of winds and
storms by Zeus.

level brine Smooth sea.

Panope One of the Nereids, sea nymphs and daughters of Neptune.

in the eclipse i.e. at an unpropitious time (eclipses were supposed to
bring evil).

with curses dark Oaths were sworn to cause misfortune to someone or
something.

Camus The River Cam, seen as a river-god.

went footing slow Passed along with heavy stride.

on the edge i.e. of the bonnet.

that sanguine flower The flower made by the mourning Apollo to
spring from the blood of his beloved Hyacinthus, with the Greek word
'ai', expressive of grief, along with the petals.

pledge Child. From the idea of its being a hostage to fortune.

Pilot St Peter, the fisherman of Galilee, leading apostle and, by
tradition, the first bishop of Rome (of which the arms are two crossed
keys). The remarks apply here to the Anglican Communion.

massy Massive.

amain With force.

for their bellies' sake For the sake of a living as a priest.

climb into the fold See John, 10,1.

Blind mouths ... sheep-hook A startling example of a mixed
metaphor. Their speech shows they are blinded by ignorance of the
simplest essentials.

have learnt aught else the least Have acquired as little knowledge as
is possible of any other subject.

What need they 'Care' is understood.

sped Appointed (to office).

list Please.

scrannel Thin, unmelodious.

the grim wolf The Roman Church.

privy paw i.e. secret conversions.

and nothing said Without protest (from the Anglican authorities).

two-handed engine Not some kind of guillotine, but, perhaps, a large sword or an axe. The sinister rhyme 'door' – 'no more' suggests instant justice.

Alpheus See note in 'Arcades', p.48.

dread voice That of Diana, who turned Arethusa into a fountain.

shrunk thy stream Caused them to find their way underground.

Sicilian Muse Theocritus, born in Syracuse in the third century BC, gave literary form to pastoral poetry in his *Idylls*.

where the mild whispers use Which the whispering sounds frequent; 'shades' are probably spirits.

lap Hollow expanse (of the valley).

swart star Sirius, or the Dog-star, which appeared at the hottest period of the year and so was the 'cause' of swarthy skins and brown vegetation.

enamell'd eyes Coloured centres that look like eyes.

such Absorb.

purple Make bright.

rathe Early.

forsaken Originally 'unwedded'. Cf. Shakespeare's 'pale primroses, That die unmarried' (The Winter's Tale, IV, 4, 122).

crow-toe Wild hyacinth.

freak'd Streaked.

must rose A rambler.

Amaranthus Classical name for 'love-lies-bleeding'.

laureate hearse The tomb of a poet. A hearse was originally a framework fixed above a tomb to hold candles. This 'tomb' is, of course, imaginary.

whelming tide Overpowering sea.

the monstrous world The ocean inhabited by sea-monsters.

to our moist vows denied i.e. our tearful entreaties to be given thy body being rejected.

by the fable of Bellerus old Off the coast of west Cornwall, known to the Romans as Belerium. This 'fabled' giant is adapted by Milton from that name.

Vision of the Guarded Mount St Michael's Mount, Cornwall, is a

romantic sight, with church and castle perched on a large rock, joined
to the mainland by a causeway submerged at high tide. The Archangel
Michael often appeared on high places (cf. Mont St Michel off the
opposite coast of France), and is said to have appeared here to the local
people. 'Guarded' may suggest the look-out at the top of the church
tower, fitted out for a lantern and called 'St Michael's Chair'.

Namancos and Bayona's hold Bayona, in the north-west corner of
Spain, near Vigo, has an ancient castle. Namancos has been found on
an old map, near Finisterre to the north. Both would have been visible
from the ship when Milton was on his way to or from Italy.

melt with ruth i.e. change from anger against possible Spanish
invaders to pity for Lycidas.

dolphins Their legendary friendliness to humans is now part of natural
history. One rescued Arion, a celebrated musician in ancient Greece,
and carried him to the shore.

Weep no more Conventional end to pastoral elegy.

your sorrow For whom you sorrow.

day star The sun.

tricks Trims.

new-spangled ore Freshly glittering gold.

mounted high i.e. resurrected.

him that walk'd the waves Christ (see Matthew, 14, 25).

other i.e. in another world.

nectar The drink of the gods.

nuptial The union of Christ with the body of believers is often referred
to in the Bible in terms of marriage. (See especially Revelations, 21).

Genius The indwelling spirit (where land meets sea).

In thy large recompense To reward you in this ample fashion.

uncouth swain Obscure shepherd.

still Quiet, i.e. before anyone was about.

Mourn Aurora, goddess of dawn, preceded the sun, hence her 'sandals
gray'.

went out Came out.

quills Reeds in his flute.

Doric lay Song in the somewhat rustic dialect of the Dorian race of
ancient Greeks, who established a colony in Syracuse in Sicily, home of
Theocritus (pastoral poet of the 3rd century BC; his verse was imitated
by Virgil).

At last He had been sitting piping all day long.

twitch'd Tugged together.

blue The colour for shepherds and other servants.

Tomorrow ... pastures new Another theme, tribute having been

paid to Lycidas. (Students will recognize this as the source of a
common saying.)

L'Allegro (OUP 17) *and Il Penseroso* (OUP 23)

These are the general favourites. They appear together like
inseparable twins, in the best anthologies of English poetry. They
are two sides of the same coin: social enjoyment and solitary
reflection, both necessary to a balanced outlook on life. In so far as
they concern Milton himself (and their lyrical quality is one of
complete self-expression), they represent not two alternatives, but
two sides of his character – before it was somewhat soured by
controversial pamphleteering. There is the objective side, eagerly
sharing cultured entertainment with congenial companions; and
the subjective side, soberly communing, alone, with spiritual
influences, reinforced by deep reading.

The two poems are remarkably symmetrical. They are of nearly
equal length (152 and 176 lines), in *octosyllabic couplets*, headed by
ten lines, alternatively *three feet* and *five feet*, rhyming abbacddeec.
This brief preamble exorcizes the opposite mood; then the poet
welcomes the chosen mood, describes the appropriate pleasures
and finally luxuriates in music selected for the occasion. Such
carefully contrived symmetry serves to highlight the contrast; the
difference between the two moods is felt also in the subtle difference
in rhythm, through skilful choice of sound and variation of stress.
In 'L'Allegro' the verse moves swiftly with a light spirit: 'Come, and
trip it as you go.' In 'Il Penseroso' it moves in stately fashion with a
solemn spirit: 'With even step and musing gait'.

The stress is mainly *iambic*, with impulsive switches to *trochaic*,
dictated largely by the first word in the line:

Énding on the rústling léaves
With mínute-dróps from off the éaves.

The contrast is not internal, but between two separate pieces of
verse, each presented as a choice. The offer remains open in both

cases, and presumably at the same time; it serves as a framework for these companion pictures of the ideal life. Certainly Contemplation and Fasting constitute an alternative way of life to Jokes and Feasting, but neither needs to be permanent.

The persistently Cheerful Man can be as wearisome as the persistently Serious Man. Neither of these poems cancels the other out, though critics may detect a bias on the poet's part towards Melancholy, in keeping with his popular image of an unsmiling Puritan, constantly justifying the ways of God to a Man more and more disinclined to listen.

However, the sensible way is to regard the two poems as interchangeable moods, like the successive seasons of the year. As summer is to winter, so is conviviality to scholarship; a person may pass from one to the other, strengthened and balanced. It is therefore the same person who in one place says 'Mirth, admit me of thy crew' and in another 'let my lamp at midnight hour/Be seen in some high lonely tower'. Choice had to be made, before long, of the course to be followed for what was to prove a period of twenty years, a choice not of temperament and amusement, but of sacrificing a life of dedication to poetic creation to one of service to the public interest. He did not hesitate.

A detailed comparison of the two poems is rewarding. In *L'Allegro* the poet is very much a spectator, looking on at various picturesque activities in rural surroundings – more picturesque no doubt to the visiting townsman than to the farm workers involved! For the poet everything from sunrise onwards is a delight. He rushes in imagination from one scene to another, from barn door to grazing sheep, from castle to cottage, from work in the fields to dancing and creepy tales at the supper table. Then the townsman has his turn, and the day's events are doubled. At the same brisk pace we look in at tournaments and poetry contests; at weddings solemnized by banquets and pageants; at the theatre with scenes of comedy: all finally submerged in the enchantment of perfect music, vocal and instrumental.

In *Il Penseroso* the poet is part of the changing scene and the scene belongs to him. There is no other human activity to look upon; he is the sole actor: I walk, I hear, I sit, my eyelids, my feet, my lamp, hide me, dissolve me, etc. The loud, breezy noises of busy humans and domestic animals are replaced by a *silent* nightingale and distant echoing sounds. The timetable is reversed; instead of progressing from dawn to dusk, we begin in the dark and return to daylight. The doubling of movement here is from outdoors to indoors: moon-gazing by the favourite oak and, when there is a nip in the air, long hours of reading by lamplight. The poet flees the morning sun to find shade in the still woods, where the humming of bees and the murmur of the stream (perhaps the 'haunted stream' of *L'Allegro*, line 130) induce him to sleep and dream. From the nymph-haunted wood with its 'archèd walks' it is a gentle, almost imperceptible transition to the 'high embowèd roof' of a Gothic choir. Finally, a young man's vision of old age as an oracle whose wisdom is based on natural knowledge.

The student will find numerous instances of what must be intentionally contrasted features. Here are a few:

L'Allegro	Il Penseroso
lark	nightingale
cock-crow	cricket on the hearth
hounds and horn	curfew
theatre	cloister
sock (comedy)	buskin (tragedy)
goddess fair	pensive nun
busy hum	mute silence
Fancy's child	the spirit of Plato

It has been suggested that 'walk unseen' ('Il Penseroso', line 65) must have been written before 'not unseen' ('L'Allegro', line 57). Was the chreerful mood an afterthought?

These poems, whose total effect is enhanced by their opposition to one another, may well have inspired many young minds to attempt the art of poetry. Natural settings; lively personification; literary and mythological allusions; vignettes of daily life; musical echoes: all are blended in two easily flowing streams of unsurpassed diction.

L'Allegro

In cheerful mood. *Themes:* Banishment of Melancholy – welcome to Mirth – her possible parentage – her companions – pleasures of morning in the countryside – harvesting at noon – supper and superstitious tales in the evening – town-life with tournaments, wedding ceremonies, masques, stage plays (comedy) – relaxing music exquisitely modulated, creating irresistible harmony.

Cerberus See *The classical element* section.

Stygian Hellish, from the River Styx, one of the four rivers of the Underworld.

forlorn Lost, desolate.

uncouth Unknown, obscure.

Darkness Erebus, married to Nox (night).

low-brow'd Overhanging.

Cimmerian The name is proverbial for darkness, from the Cimmerii, a piratical race who lived in the caves where they stored their plunder.

y-cleped Called, named (Archaic).

Euphrosyne One of the three Graces, daughters of Venus.

at a birth i.e. triplets.

Two sister Graces Aglaia and Thalia.

Bacchus God of wine and festivity (see notes on *Comus*). The ivy was one of the plants sacred to him.

sager i.e. knowing better (accounts vary).

Zephyr The West Wind.

a-maying Gathering flowers in May.

buxom Comely (and, today, plump).

debonair Gracious.

Quips Witty remarks.

Cranks Fanciful expressions, perhaps deliberate twistings of meanings.

wanton Wiles Mischievous tricks.

Becks Gestures.

wreathèd Describing the puckering of a smiling face.

Hebe A goddess who was always in the bloom of youth.

mountain-nymph i.e. finding her last refuge in the mountains.

unreprovèd Innocent.

dappled Marked with dark and light spots; used of horses, to come in spite of sorrow. This must be the poet at his own window, brushing sorrow aside and greeting the new day.

Straight Immediately afterwards.

fallows Ploughlands without crops.

trim Neat (because mown for hay).

pied Variegated (here, green with white).

Towers and battlements Horton is about five miles from Windsor.

lies i.e. dwells.

Cynosure Centre of attraction.

Corydon and Thyrsis The names of imaginary shepherds used by classical poets. Similarly, Phyllis (here, Phillis) and Thestylis are country girls.

messes Dishes.

earlier i.e. before the autumn harvest.

upland Well inland.

rebecks Early fiddles.

chequer'd shade Mixed sunlight and shadow.

come i.e. who have come.

fairy Mab Legendary fairy appearing in works of Shakespeare and other poets.

junkets Delicacies (originally of cream), now made from milk and sugar, with added rennet.

She ... he Two who are telling their experiences.

Friar's Lantern Correctly, Jack o' Lantern, a will-o'-the-wisp or flickering flame caused by marsh gas which misled travellers. Not easily connected with what follows.

the drudging goblin sweat The sprite, slaving away at his task, sweated.

lubber fiend Ghostly scullion, known as 'Lob-lie-by-the-fire'.

chimney's length The width of the fireplace.

weeds of peace i.e. civilian garments.

triumphs Public displays.

Rain influence Inspire (to greater efforts).

wit or arms i.e. literary composition or jousts.

both i.e. contestants in both arts.

her grace i.e. the Queen's favour.

Hymen Greek god whose presence was essential at every marriage, wearing a purple robe and holding a lighted torch and the nuptial veil of saffron.

clear Not smoking.

anon At once.

Jonson's learnèd sock Ben Jonson (1572–1637), great writer of comedies with a reputation for learning even among the University wits. The 'soccus' was worn by actors in classical times to indicate comedy: it was a light shoe, different from the 'buskin' of tragedy.

Fancy's child i.e. genius gifted with imagination.

native wood-notes wild Shakespeare's plays have a number of rural scenes, but 'wild' probably refers gently to his comparative lack of classical education.

Lydian Tender. From the Lydian mode in Greek music.

meeting soul Responsive mind.

a winding bout ... long drawn out Prolonged passage of intricate and unceasing sweetness of tone.

wanton heed and giddy cunning Extravagant care and intoxicated skill. A double oxymoron.

mazes Bewildering turns.

hidden i.e. unheard until released.

Orpheus See *The classical element*.

Elysian Elysium was the paradise of the ancients.

Il Penseroso

In serious mood (mod. Italian *pensieroso*). *Themes*: Banishment of Mirth – welcome to Melancholy – her parents – her companions – outdoor walks in the moonlight to hear the nightingale or the distant curfew – indoor late-night sessions in a firelit room – midnight hours reading philosophy, Greek tragedy, Chaucer's Tales and chivalric lays – morning sunlight after chilly start – shady woods where the only sound is the murmur of a stream, there to dream and wake to music – spiritual ecstasy in college chapel – last scene of all, prophetic utterances in a hermit's grotto.

without father bred i.e. lacking a father's discipline. Folly is a personification, not a mythical being.

bestead Are of use.

fill i.e. how little you fill.

fixèd mind Mind resolved upon its goal in life.

fancies fond ... possess Fill silly imaginations with bright apparitions.

hovering dreams Floating visions.

fickle pensioners of Morpheus' train Unreliable favourites in the retinue of the god of dreams, Morpheus (from Greek word 'to give shape to').

Melancholy One of the four 'humours' once regarded as conditioning human temperament. Here the mood is of solemn reflection. The cheerful mood of *L'Allegro* would be due to the 'sanguine' humour.

To hit the sense i.e. to be caught by the faculty.

our weaker view Our visionary power too weak (for such brightness). An unusual aspect of melancholy.

staid Wisdom's hue The colour best suited to the gravity of wisdom.

Prince Memnon's sister She mourned her brother Memnon, a king of

Ethiopia (not to be confused with Agamemnon, king of Mycenae, leader of the Greeks in the siege of Troy). Memnon helped the Trojans against the Greeks and was killed by Achilles. His name was falsely attached to a colossal statue of a Pharaoh near Thebes in Egypt.

starr'd Ethiop queen Cassiopeia (now a constellation) boasted that she was fairer than the Nereids, whereupon Neptune sent a monster to ravage Ethiopia. Her daughter, Andromeda, was rescued from Ethiopia by Perseus.

higher far descended The descendant of far higher creatures, i.e. gods. This descent is of Milton's creation.

Vesta Goddess of the hearth (hence 'bright-haired') and daughter of Saturn. Her worship in Rome was maintained by four virgin priestesses, the Vestals.

solitary Saturn Father of Jupiter; Saturn devoured his other sons (hence 'solitary'). Jupiter (Jove), who had been hidden by his mother, replaced him as king of the gods.

Ida's inmost grove The heavily wooded mountain range in Asia Minor called Mount Ida was frequented by the gods. Jupiter grew up on another Mount Ida in Crete.

darkest grain Deepest shade of dye, violet or purple.

sable stole of cypress lawn Black shawl made of a fine transparent material that originated in Cyprus.

commercing with the skies Communicating with Heaven.

Muses Goddesses of the arts, daughters of Jupiter, with whom they were associated in some Greek festivals.

retirèd Secluded, away from busy streets.

yon Yonder.

Cherub One of the second order of angels. For the throne, see Ezekiel 10.

hist along Summon with a 'hist'.

Less Unless, i.e. breaking the silence.

Philomel The nightingale. For her story see section on *The classical element*.

Cynthia Diana (born on Mount Cynthus), goddess of hunting and the moon. Her chariot was pulled by two white stags, whereas that of Hecate, goddess of the underworld (and identified with Diana) had dragons.

accustom'd oak His own?

woo Pay court to, entreat.

missing thee In thy absence.

highest noon The place of the moon at midnight.

bow'd The impression given by passing clouds.

plat A small patch.

curfew Evening bell (originally for extinguishing fires).

wide-water'd Suggesting a long coast-line, corresponding to the remoteness of the sound.

Swinging slow with sullen roar The alliteration of sibilants adds to the sound effect of the waves, with pauses between the breakers.

air i.e. the cold air of winter.

removèd Out of the way.

counterfeit a gloom Produce an imperfect kind of darkness.

bellman's drowsy charm ... harm The monotonous sound of the night-watchman's voice as he goes his rounds, calling out 'Past one o'clock', etc., and calling for the protection of those asleep.

the Bear The Great Bear, a constellation.

With thrice-great Hermes i.e. studying, like some of Milton's contemporaries, the works of 'Hermes Trismegistos' (Greek 'tris', thrice, 'megistos', greatest), the presumed author of Platonic-type writings enshrining much ancient Egyptian teaching.

unsphere Detach from his place in the sky (to reveal the truth about the after life on which he speculated when on earth).

The immortal mind i.e. of individual men after death. The *god* Hermes (Roman Mercury) and the Egyptian Thoth were concerned with the arrival of the dead in the underworld.

nook Small corner, i.e. the earth in comparison with the universe.

daemons Spirits: salamanders in fire, sylphs in the air, nymphs in the water and gnomes underground – then regarded as the four main elements.

true consent Perfect co-operation: with 'planet', astrology; with 'element', scientific knowledge.

sceptred pall Royal robe, the *wearer* carrying the sceptre.

Thebes Oedipus, king of this Greek city, was the chief character in tragedies by Sophocles. Pelops was the ancestor of Agamemnon and other Greek chiefs.

Troy divine The ten years' war between the Trojans and the besieging Greeks provided several plots. Neptune was said to have built the walls.

Ennobled hath the buskin'd stage i.e. good recent tragedies. The buskin was a high-heeled boot worn by Greek tragic actors.

Musaeus A very early Greek poet of whom nothing has survived. His 'bower', a small room to which to retire, is a favourite word with Milton.

iron tears Pluto, god of the underworld, was a grim figure; he was also called Hades (Hell).

him that left half told Geoffrey Chaucer (1340–1400), one of whose

Canterbury Tales, that of the Squire, stops halfway or, rather, is tactfully interrupted by the Franklin.

Camball ... Algarsife ... Canace The two sons and daughter of a Tartar king, Cambus Khan.

virtuous ring and glass The ring and mirror were sent by the King of Arabia to Canace. The 'virtue' (magic power) of the ring was to make bird language intelligible, and of the mirror to reflect deceit in others.

wondrous horse of brass A mechanical wonder for the king himself: it would transport him where he liked within the space of a day.

Of forests and enchantments drear This suggests the reading of Spenser's *Faerie Queene*, full of allegory, in which 'more is meant than meets the ear'.

pale career Moonlit journey.

civil-suited Wearing everyday dress.

frounced With her hair curled.

Attic boy Cephalus, son of a king of Thessaly, married Procris, daughter of a king of Athens (whence 'Attic'). The dawn goddess Aurora's infatuation for Cephalus led to the tragic death of Procris, who, consumed with jealousy, hid in a bush to spy on her husband. Cephalus, thinking he heard a wild animal, threw his javelin and killed Procris. Overwhelmed by grief, Cephalus killed himself.

Sylvan Roman rustic god, half man, half goat, frequenting the woods.

such consort as they keep i.e. their kind of music.

dewy-feather'd sleep The god Somnus (Sleep) in one of his representations is winged, dropping slumber like dew from his feathers.

Wave at his wings Be borne on his wings.

embowèd Vaulted.

antic pillars massy proof Piers of a nave supporting the solid weight of walls and roof, with ancient carvings on their capitals.

storied windows richly dight Windows fitted with beautiful stained glass illustrating sacred events.

strain Utterance.

At a Solemn Music (**OUP** 15)

Let poetic song inspire the human race with the desire to join in the heavenly harmony that characterizes the universe.

Sirens Enchantresses, like the Sirens.

Sphere-born Born of the celestial spheres.

Voice and Verse Song and Poetry (the above 'Sirens').

mix'd power Blended strength.

with inbreathed sense With life breathed into them.

high-raised phantasy Stimulated imagination.

undisturbèd Calm.

concent Harmony.

saintly i.e. uttered by saints (believers).

Seraphim Together with the Cherubim, these were the highest orders of angels, specially charged with attendance on God.

burning Shining.

That we on Earth Clause of purpose depending on the verbs in line 3.

undiscording Free from discords.

noise Music (and nothing discordant about it).

In first obedience In their original state of obedience (which Man forsook).

consort Concert.

endless morn of light i.e. continual dawn and no darkness.

On Time (OUP 14)

Time is called upon to hasten towards its end and so lead to an eternal life of goodness and happiness, with freedom from bondage to events on earth.

envious Grudging, malicious. Here, *either* grudging, by its slow movement, the events that are to happen, *or* jealously destroying everything it overtakes.

Whose speed ... pace The rate of whose passing is controlled by the ponderous movement of the pendulum. A reference in one manuscript suggests that this poem was written for a clock.

glut thyself ... devours Choke yourself (in such haste) with all the things that are swallowed up in your stomach.

false and vain i.e. things temporal.

mortal dross Perishable scum (impure metal).

whenas When once.

t'whose happy-making sight alone i.e. confronted solely by the vision that brings bliss. At this point the involved sentence structure collapses: two subordinate clauses are crushed into one – 'to whose happy-making sight alone our heavenly-guided soul shall climb' and 'When once our heavenly-guided soul shall climb to His happy-making sight alone'.

The sonnet

This lyric of fourteen lines of *iambic pentameter* was only one of a score of stanzas originating in Renaissance Italy, but it survived them all to become the recognized form of expression for a single idea or emotion. Its brevity and rhyming pattern gave it an epigrammatic quality; its one sheet of paper was easily passed from hand to hand, sometimes anonymously. It could embody deep feeling or rank simply as an exercise in conventional poetic diction.

In the last decade of the reign of Elizabeth I, following the appearance of those of the sonnets of Sidney and Spenser, it was all the rage to address love poems to one particular lady, between whom and the poet there might be a social or marital barrier. Nothing reflects the significance of the sonnet more than that our greatest poet himself produced 152 (repeatedly researched by scholars in attempts to identify his noble patron, and the dark-haired mistress!). Shakespeare's sonnets will always by shrouded in mystery, but something is revealed of the otherwise almost entirely hidden nature of the playwright who projected such a gallery of human characters on to the contemporary stage.

The Elizabethan or Shakespearian sonnet was arranged as three rhyming *quatrains*, closed by a rhyming *couplet*. Thus the climax, where there was one, came at the end. Milton, who could read, speak and write verse in Italian, introduced the Italian, or Petrarchan form, named after Francesco Petrarca (1304–74), who wrote three hundred sonnets to 'Laura'. In the hands of Milton and his followers it consisted of an *octave*, a descriptive exposition, followed by a *sestet*, which resolved the question or announced a decision – in so far as such a general rule can be deduced from a collection of what are essentially occasional poems. In Milton's sonnets the fair sex, object of honest admiration and not a desperate lover's passion, is overshadowed by literary, political and social matters.

The rhyme-scheme is more involved than that of the Elizabethan: the *octave* in two linked *quatrains*, rhyming abbaabba; the *sestet* in two separate or linked *tercets*, rhyming variously, some with three rhymes, some with only two, e.g. cddcdc. In this form the climax is central, somewhere in the transition from *octave* to *sestet*. In some the break in sense between lines 8 and 9 is abrupt, in others it is spread out over two or three lines. Milton rarely uses the sharp turn (the sonnet on Fairfax has an example); in the two powerful sonnets, the Massacre and the Blindness, there is a climax at the transition, but with *enjambment* – i.e. the sense of line 8 is completed in line 9.

The example set by Milton's sonnets was away from exuberant fancy and extravagant sentiments to practical considerations, illustrated or symbolized by personifications, mythological allusions or familiar metaphors. The poet himself occupies a central position, dispensing praise or blame, admiration or condemnation, warnings or prayers for vengeance. They might be classified as verse epistles, loftier versions than those vitriolic letters addressed to various opponents.

Milton's sonnets were largely ignored in the following century, but received a dramatic revival immediately after Dorothy Wordsworth read some of them to her brother. William seized his pen and started on the production of what eventually became several volumes of sonnets, some of them attacking with Miltonic zest the enemies of freedom in the Europe of Napoleon. And he had occasion to look back on his great predecessor:

'Scorn not the Sonnet, Critic, you have frowned,
Mindless of its just honours . . .
. . . when a damp
Fell round the path of Milton, in his hand
The Thing became a trumpet; whence he blew
Soul-animating strains – alas, too few!'

The twenty or so – their limited number reflecting the careful revision given to all his verse – mostly cover the twenty-year period when poetic composition was put aside for other tasks. Perhaps they provided an outlet for artistic creation in miniature, as some relief from the prose harangues in support of official policies. The sonnets are truly 'occasional', dealing with a variety of topics, though in their published order they seem to pair themselves off: two on ladies, two on ignorant critics, two on Parliamentary leaders, two on innocent victims, two on modest dissipations.

Sonnet summaries and textual notes
(OUP 91–105)

To the nightingale

An appeal to the nightingale to be heard this year before the cuckoo, and so promise success in love.

While the holly hours ... May While the blithe Seasons usher in the month of May, favourable to lovers.
Now timely sing Sing in good time (before the cuckoo).
the rude bird of hate i.e. the vulgar symbol of marital discord (cuckold: husband of an unfaithful wife).
too late ... relief i.e. not in time to obtain for me any solace (for my pain).
no reason why i.e. no reason for betraying me.
Whether the Muse ... his mate Whichever of these two you represent, I serve both of them.

On His being Arrived to the Age of Twenty-Four

A vow that whatever the delay over its appearance, his work will be a fulfilment.

the subtle thief of youth i.e. Time imperceptibly steals the years away.
my late spring i.e. my delayed production of (published) poetry.
my semblance My outward appearance.
deceive the truth Give a false impression.
inward ripeness Maturity of mind.
That some ... endu'th Which (ripeness) is bestowed upon those more fortunate in showing it (a possible reference to some contemporaries).
even ... high Proportionate to that career, whether it be a humble or a prominent one.
As ever ... eye As if being continuously observed by God (who has imposed on me the task of writing great poetry).

When the Assault was Intended to the City

A plea (only half-serious) to those Royalists who threaten to take and sack London, to spare his dwelling – that of a poet who can confer immortality on them.

Colonel Three syllables. From the Italian word for the commander of a column.

Whose chance ... may seize Whose fortune it may be to take possession of this house of mine (outside the City walls).

harms Injury by soldiery engaged in sacking.

charms The necessary poetic incantations (magic power of verse).

clime Region (poetic).

bright circle Circling *of the earth* with its rays.

spear This (by then) archaic weapon serves as a link between the seventeenth century and ancient Greece.

the Muses' bower i.e. Milton's house.

The great Emathian conqueror Alexander III (356–323 BC), whose dynasty came from Emathia, a province in Macedonia, sacked Thebes for revolting against him; he spared only the house of its famous poet Pindarus, who died 435 BC.

sad Electra's poet Euripides (480–406 BC), author of *Electra* and a number of other plays that have survived, was described by Aristotle as 'the most tragic of the poets'. Electra arranged for her brother to kill their mother in revenge for the murder of their father. The Spartan general who had Athens at his mercy is said to have spared the city on hearing lines from this play.

To a Virtuous Young Lady

To an unknown young lady whose virtue has made others scornful in their jealousy.

the broad way and the green See Matthew, 7,13: 'broad is the way that leadeth to destruction'. 'Green', if not merely a rhyming word, suggests either pleasant walking or the full vigour of the senses.

eminently Conspicuously.

ruth Pity. There is identical rhyme here, though one is a proper noun.

Thy care is fix'd Thy concern (about spiritual things) is immovable.

odorous Sweet-smelling (from the good deeds that fuel the lamp).

feastful Festive.

To the Lady Margaret Ley

To the daughter of a nobleman of distinction who reminds the poet of her father, not only in her words, but in her own character. *Octave*: the character of the Earl; *sestet*: repeated in his daughter.

that good Earl James Ley became Lord Chief Justice in 1621 and Lord High Treasurer in 1624. Charles I created him Earl of Marlborough and transferred him to the Presidency of the Council. He died in 1629, soon after Charles's Dissolution of Parliament.

fee Wealth, especially in land. Here probably 'bribe'. He pronounced sentence on Sir Francis Bacon for bribe taking.

more in himself content Preferring his own company or, possibly, liking better to live on his own resources.

breaking Suspension.

dishonest victory The victory of the autocratic Philip of Macedon over the democratic Greek forces at Chaeronea was regarded by the poet as 'dishonest' (dishonourable).

fatal to liberty Taking away the freedom of the Athenians and their allies.

that old man eloquent The Greek orator Isocrates (436–338 BC).

On the Detraction which followed upon my Writing certain Treatises

Those who are put off by strange words from the Greek are unworthy successors of a more scholarly generation.

Tetrachordon The Greek name for a musical instrument with *four* strings. The uninitiated could hardly be blamed for not recognizing in this term the *harmonizing* of four scriptural passages on marriage and divorce: Genesis, 1,27–8; Genesis, 2,18 and 23–4; Deuteronomy, 14,1–2; Matthew, 5, 31–2 and 19,3–11; Corinthians, 7, 10–11.

woven close Carefully written.

The subject new ... intellects While the topic was fresh (introduced by Milton himself), it circulated in the town for a while, counting among its readers some good intellects.

spelling false Misunderstanding it, or simply unable to pronounce the word.

Mile-End Green This part of London gets its name from the first milestone out of Aldgate – therefore quite a distance to walk, certainly from where Milton lived in Aldersgate Street.

Gordon ... Galasp Any Scottish names would serve here! The first three were officers concerned in the temporary alliance of Charles I with the Scots; the fourth was a Covenanter.

our like mouths i.e. the poet's contemporaries have grown accustomed to making harsh noises.

grow sleek Become smooth by frequent use.

Quintilian Quintilian Marcus Fabius (d. AD 95). Teacher of oratory and composer of a system for perfect public-speaking: it included warnings against staring and gasping.

soul of Sir John Cheek The spirit of a professor of Greek at the University, and tutor to King Edward VI.

Hated not learning ... asp This break in sense is possibly due to a faulty merging of two constructions: 'not worse than our generation does' and 'hated learning worse than toad or asp'. Reptiles have long been objects of hatred.

On the Same

Contemporary ideas about liberty are hypocritical; the critics of his pamphlets on divorce howl at the freedom which divorce can bring to unhappy partners, and they clamour for the licensing of publications in order to suppress the very Liberty for which they have been fighting.

quit their clogs Get rid of their encumbrances (originally weights attached to the legs of animals to prevent their straying).

known rules of ancient liberty Familiar principles of freedom as practised, for example, among the early Hebrews.

Of owls and cuckoos ... dogs This sweeping line envisages a hostile crowd that includes five types: the ignorant, the ungrateful, the stupid, the mockers and the backbiters. The rhyming word links up with frogs and hogs. Theological disputants in the seventeenth century were almost as free with derogatory labels as some political propagandists in the twentieth.

those hinds The peasants in Lycia (a country of Asia Minor) who abused Latona (goddess and mother, by Jupiter, of the twins Apollo and Diana), when, in flight from the wrath of Juno, she stopped to ask them for water. To punish them she turned them into frogs by the edge of the lake they were weeding.

after held the sun and moon in fee When they grew up they
  possessed the sun (Apollo) and moon (Diana).

pearl to hogs From Matthew, 7,6: 'neither cast ye your pearls before
  swine, lest they trample them under their feet.' The use of the singular
  'pearl' suggests the substance, i.e. valuable writings.

waste of wealth and loss of blood A reference to the destruction and
  slaughter in the Civil War, then in its last stages.

To Mr Henry Lawes, on His Airs

Henry Lawes set Milton's poetry and that of some of his contemporaries to music, so skilfully that in return he deserves to be
celebrated in verse.

Harry This familiar address to a man twelve years older and a
  royalist shows this must have been a friendship over a long period.

well-measured In correct rhythm. Lawes's musical accompaniments
  brought out the qualities of the verse, something more than fitting
  the words to the tune.

span Measure (and so link meaning and music together).

just note and accent Right sound and stress.

scan Indicate the metre by marking the arrangement of long and
  short vowels – in classical verse – or of stressed and unstressed
  syllables (in English verse).

Midas' ears This king of Phrygia preferred the music of Pan to
  that of Apollo and was punished by being given an ass's ears.

exempts Distinguishes.

to look wan Paleness was considered a mark of envy.

with smooth air With refined melody.

humour best our tongue Adapt his music to English speech.

priest of Pheobus' quire Comparing Lawes to a priest at Apollo's
  oracle, assisting poets who come for inspiration.

happiest Most effective.

Dante Dante Alighieri (1265–1321); in Part 2 of the *Divina Commedia*,
  Canto 2, lines 76–117, Dante describes his brief meeting in his journey
  through Purgatory with an old and intimate friend who on earth set some
  of the poet's lyrics to music. When asked by Dante to sing something,
  he chooses one of these lyrics, but the poet is not allowed to hear him
  finish it.

milder Either than other parts of Purgatory, or than the Inferno (Hell).

On the Religious Memory of Mrs Catharine Thomason, my Christian Friend, Deceased December, 1646.

A departed soul whose virtuous acts on earth will be her companions in the bliss of eternity.

Faith and Love This is a sonnet of personifications: Life; Death; handmaids.

thee Mrs Catharine Thomason was brought up by her uncle, a bookseller, and she married George Thomason, also a bookseller, who collected tracts and pamphlets to the number of some 22,000. They include some of Milton's and are now in the British Museum.

this earthy load ... doth sever The mortal body – in which we are dead though we think we are alive – that separates us from eternal life.

purple Brightly coloured.

On the New Forcers of Conscience under the Long Parliament (OUP 98)

This (Italian) form of the sonnet is longer than the Elizabethan 14-line sonnet; a 3-line *coda* is added on at the end – more than one set of three lines being added at will.

A protest against the proposed replacement of one ecclesiastical tyranny (the Church of England) by another (the Assembly of Divines, mostly Presbyterian) and a warning that Parliament will not tolerate the substitution of Presbyterian elder for Anglican priest.

Prelate Lord The Anglican bishop.

stiff Resolute.

Liturgy Form of church worship, here the Anglican Prayer Book.

Plurality Holding more than one parish or church office; 'widowed' – an unusual state for a loose woman to be in – means that there are no more priests enjoying this privilege.

envied Implying that the Presbyterians were also zealous office-seekers.

Dare ye ... consciences Have you the impertinence to call upon the authorities to impose uniformity of belief on our minds? The advocates of a form of Presbyterian church government were called 'New Forcers'.

hierarchy Body of priests in order of superiority: still used in a derogatory sense. By 'classic' is probably meant the 'classis', or 'presbytery', consisting of a number of congregations, rather like a present rural deanery.

mere A.S. Dr Adam Stuart, a Presbyterian opponent of the Independents, with whom Milton was now in sympathy.

Rotherford Samuel Rutherford (not Rotherford), a member of the Assembly and a noted heresy-hunter. Both these men were professors, at Leyden and St Andrews respectively.

Men whose life ... with Paul i.e. Independents, of whom there were five in the Assembly.

Edwards Thomas Edwards, preacher and pamphleteer.

What-d'ye-call Robert Baillie, a Scottish Commissioner. We now use 'What's-his-name' for someone of minor importance in our eyes.

packings Intrigues.

Trent The Council of Trent, called by the Roman Church to counteract Protestantism.

phylacteries Boxes of Hebrew texts inscribed on vellum worn on their foreheads by Jews at prayer to show their piety. To Christ a token of Pharisaic hypocrisy.

baulk your ears Avoid (clipping) your ears.

When they shall read ... charge When they (those who fear) shall see this (the next line) printed in the charge to be made against you.

Priest This word is a derivation through Old English 'preost' and Latin 'presbyter', from the Greek 'presbiteros', an elder or chieftain, which was used for the earliest form of assistant to a bishop. Presbyterian church officers are now Elders.

On the Lord General Fairfax, at the Siege of Colchester

The man who first led Parliamentary forces to victory is faced by the domestic task of dealing with corruption in the Commonwealth.

Fairfax Thomas Fairfax, the third Baron (1612–71) was the victor of Naseby and put down the royalist 'rebellion' in 1648. He captured Colchester after stubborn resistance by the king's supporters.

false North Scottish forces formerly on the Parliamentary side invaded England on behalf of Charles, thus breaking the Solemn League and Covenant, but were defeated at Preston by Cromwell.

imp Graft fresh feathers on to a damaged wing (in falconry).

their serpent wings i.e. the strength of the 'new rebellions'.

public faith A name for loans raised by Parliament.

To the Lord General Cromwell, on the Proposals of certain Ministers at the Committee for Propagation of the Gospel. May 16, 1652

The Lord Protector himself, after his decisive victories in the final stage of the war, must now conquer those who would stifle freedom of conscience.

detractions rude Coarse personal criticisms.
the neck of crownèd Fortune An indirect allusion to the execution of Charles three years before.
Darwen stream At Preston, scene of the first victory over the Scots in 1648, the second being at Dunbar in 1650 and the third at Worcester in 1651.
imbrued Dyed.
new foes The Presbyterians in Parliament and the divines were seeking to impose a new national Church after their own devising.
whose Gospel is their maw Who believe only in what they can seize for themselves: 'maw', the stomach of an animal.

To Sir Henry Vane the Younger

A leading intellectual on the Parliamentary side who served well as negotiator and organizer, but quarrelled with Cromwell over his dissolution of Parliament and who was – after the Restoration – to be tragically put to death as a Regicide, though he had disapproved of the execution of the king. He was forty-nine.

Vane, young in years His father, Sir Henry Vane the Elder, held a prominent position at the court of Charles I; he later acquired Raby Castle in Durham, where the family still live. Through a quarrel he went over to the side of Parliament. The son, Sir Henry Vane the Younger, went even farther as a republican and Puritan. A friend of Cromwell, he attacked him boldly for his acts of despotism. Said the 'Lord Protector': 'The Lord deliver me from Sir Harry Vane!'
gowns, not arms i.e. the togas worn by the Roman Senate, not the weapons of the army. In other words, negotiations, not battles.
The fierce Epirot Pyrrhus, King of Epirus, who won brilliant but costly victories. When he sued Rome for peace, his ambassador brought back a refusal and a description of the Roman Senate as an assembly of kings.

the African bold Hannibal (247–183 BC), the Carthaginian general, who carried the war with Rome into Italy by crossing the Alps. As he also, at a critical point, offered peace terms, there may be a reference here to the Dutch offer in 1652.

unfold ... hollow states Find out the real aims, under their diplomatic smoke-screen, of countries with whom they were negotiating.

hard to be spell'd Not easy to understand.

upheld i.e. if decided upon.

nerves Sinews (original meaning).

iron and gold Weapons and cash.

The bounds of either sword i.e. the limitations on each of these authorities.

On the late Massacre in Piemont

A call to God to avenge the frightful massacre of the Waldensians, a Protestant sect, in a campaign organized from Turin by the Council of the Propagation of the Faith.

Avenge, O Lord, thy slaughtered saints Founded by Peter Waldo of Lyon in the twelfth century, the Waldensians (or Vaudois) had an independent form of worship – mainly prayer and Bible reading. They lived for centuries in the upper valleys of the Alps in Savoy and Piedmont, ruled by the Dukes of Savoy; and in the French province of the Dauphiny. Periodically persecuted in heretic-hunting raids, some of them suffered most dramatically in 1655 when their enemies, unable to take their mountain refuges by assault, tricked them by a false promise of peace into admitting Piedmontese soldiers into their settlements. There ensued a massacre far more terrible than Glencoe. Europe was shocked, but no action was taken on the Waldensians' behalf. Milton's opening line has become a trumpet voluntary for the world's oppressed.

thy book The Book of Life.

Piemontese Soldiers of the Duke of Savoy, who was also Prince of Piedmont; they included French and exiled Irish.

sow Scatter (imperative).

sway Rule.

The triple Tyrant The Pope, from the three crowns in his tiara.

thy way Faith in God.

the Babylonian woe The Roman Catholic Church was alluded to by the Puritans as Babylon, once capital of an empire and proverbial for wickedness.

On His Blindness

The well-known sonnet on his blindness (title supplied by others). His sight was failing for over eight years, from 1644 to 1652.

my light is spent My sight has gone (used up).
ere half my days 'Have passed' is understood.
one talent An allusion to the parable of the talents (see Matthew, 15, 14–30). The two servants who doubled the money left in their trust by their master were rewarded on his return from a long journey, whereas the cautious servant who merely hoarded his was punished.
Lodged with me useless Placed in my charge but unproductive.
more bent More eager (for being handicapped).
therewith i.e. by exercising my (poetic) talent.
fondly Foolishly.
to prevent ... murmur To anticipate my complaint.
They also serve ... wait i.e. those who are fated to go nowhere but simply act as attendants are rendering service equal to that of those given important commissions. There was considerable diplomatic activity when this sonnet was written.

To Edward Lawrence

Edward Lawrence, a young man of great promise who died in 1657 at the age of twenty-three, is invited to dinner, now that the weather is wet, instead of the usual walk. Congenial conversation and music will follow.

virtuous Possessing many good qualities and talents.
father Henry Lawrence, Lord President of the Council.
Favonius A gentle breeze from the west, bringing spring.
reinspire Breathe new life into.
neither sow'd nor spun See Matthew 6, 28: 'Consider the lilies of the field, how they grow; they toil not, neither do they spin.'
neat Tastefully prepared.
Attic taste Classic elegance.
artful voice Voice skilled in the art of singing.

Tuscan air Song from Tuscany, then a grand duchy in the centre of
Italy, with Florence as its capital.

judge i.e. tell good from bad.

spare/To interpose them oft Either (i) refrain from indulging in
them frequently, or (ii) arrange to introduce them as a diversion (from
solemn matters).

To Cyriack Skinner

Cyriack Skinner is similarly invited to spare time from more serious
matters in which to relax – something Heaven has ordained.

Cyriack A lawyer and member of Lincoln's Inn; possibly a former pupil
and certainly a friend in need to the blind poet.

grandsire Cyriack was the son of the daughter of Sir Edward Coke,
Chief Justice of the King's Bench, whose *Institutes* is a classic, famous
nationally and internationally.

Themis Goddess of Justice, represented in statues holding a sword in
one hand and scales in the other (as above the Central Criminal Court,
London).

others ... wrench Others, pleading a case, so often twist to suit it; or
other judges interpret wrongly.

deep thoughts ... draws Decide with me to drown weighty problems
in laughter that is not afterwards a cause for regret.

Euclid Greek mathematician (450–380 BC) who taught in Alexandria,
300 BC. His name was given to a school text-book based upon his
Elements of Geometry, now superseded by modern systems.

Archimedes Greek mathematician (287–212 BC) who made some
notable scientific discoveries.

what the Swede ... the French i.e. political discussions on possible
developments abroad.

disapproves that care ... refrains Is opposed to that kind of
seriousness which, while outwardly prudent, fills every minute with
unnecessary attention to duty and refuses to take any opportunity
offered to relax in company.

To the Same

The poet himself is here the theme. For him, blindness has been
ordained; it is endured in the knowledge that his sight has been lost
in defending Liberty, in tracts that have won recognition throughout Europe.

this three years' day This day three years ago.

clear ... spot Free, to all external appearance, of any fault.

Bereft of light ... forgot Deprived of the light of day, they have lost the faculty of vision.

orbs Eyeballs.

The conscience ... overplied The awareness of having lost the sight of my eyes by overtaxing them (in Liberty's defence).

from side to side From end to end.

vain mask Empty stage play (e.g. masque).

no better guide i.e. religion.

On His Deceased Wife

Sight returns to him in a dream of his dead wife coming to greet him in another world, but he wakes to the reality of his blindness. Which wife is this? Is the dream a real one or a literary invention characteristic of the sonnet?

my late espousèd saint Mary Powell died in 1652, three days after the birth of a daughter; Katherine Woodcock died in 1657 in childbirth. This latest of the sonnets could be about either 'deceased wife'. The word 'saint' was a Puritan title for any believer.

Alcestis In the drama by Euripides she saved her husband from death at the hands of his enemies by offering her life in exchange.

Jove's great son Hercules, who wrestled with Death to rescue Alcestis from the grave and restore her to her (undeserving) husband.

as whom ... taint As one purified after childbirth according to Hebraic law.

veil'd Perhaps from the custom for women in church after childbirth, or it may be (if it was his second wife) because he had never seen her face.

to my fancied sight In my dream, I could see.

inclined Leant forward.

I waked, she fled ... the night The simplest words express the deepest pathos.

Samson Agonistes

The duality of Milton's poetry – the interwoven strands of classical literature and Hebrew scripture – is nowhere more striking than in this 'choral drama' arranged, not for the stage, but for private perusal. The matter is Hebrew, the form is Greek. The panoply of a tragedy performed, as it were, in ancient Athens is set before the eyes of the religious reformer in his study in 17th-century England. He sees God's plan realized, with dramatic suddenness, at the end of a play. Throughout several episodes His chosen champion, blinded through his own folly, is roused from the depths of despair to bring about the destruction of far more of the nation's enemies by a single stroke than could have been achieved in any other way.

In his early days Milton had drawn up a long list of heroes for possible treatment in an epic poem or historic drama. Gradually, like the dawning in Samson of his great resolve, Milton came to concentrate the last mental energies of his life on this amazing parallel with his own position: blindness (for different reasons), marital unhappiness, the triumph of political enemies after years of service, even of sacrifice. His own life's task had been performed, a *magnum opus* that placed him second only to Shakespeare: *Paradise Lost* (over ten thousand lines of blank verse) and *Paradise Regained* (over two thousand). The work was composed direct from his mind, unable as he was to consult books or notes unless they were read to him; and relying upon dictation, line by line, to members of a not always sympathetic family. This was the intellectual feat that did indeed impress his contemporaries of all persuasions – like Samson's juggling before the jeering Philistines. He did not follow up by 'bringing down the house' with a performance in public by professional actors of the fate of the Israelite champion. He had read his favourite Euripides at home and college: it was text, not utterance, that he had studied in the Greek. So, disclaiming any connection with the stage of the day (one of which he saw little to approve), he produced something unique – a play in the Greek manner on a biblical subject, intended for perusal only.

Two Puritans

The publication of *Samson Agonistes* was a symbolical final triumph over religious foes, and an encouragement to those of Milton's beliefs who suffered the repressive discrimination of Acts of Parliament. It was to be followed in a few years by another challenge of a quite different literary kind: the story in the plainest prose of a representative believer finding his way to Heaven after a perilous journey through the evils and temptations of this world. For *The Pilgrim's Progress* (1678) John Bunyan drew on the people and places of his native Bedfordshire, and was influenced by several years of preaching. His work took shape in the confinement of a local prison.

Milton's imagination drew on the mythology of the Ancients and the Chronicles of the Hebrews, and was intensified by several years of scholarly study. His work took shape in the physical confinement of blindness, a prison house as absolute as that of his hero. Both writers, in their world of strong reaction to the policies of the Commonwealth government, held out to the newly oppressed the vision of ultimate triumph. Bunyan followed Christian with his eyes: 'behold, the City shone like the sun, the streets also were paved with gold, and in them walked many men with crowns on their heads.' The leader of Milton's Chorus waxes lyrical: 'O dearly bought revenge, yet glorious!/Living or dying thou hast fulfilled/ The work for which thou wast foretold/To Israel, and now liest victorious/Among thy slain self-killed.' Christian enters into immortal life; Samson's immortality is the preservation of his memory and the inscribed record of his deeds. Not for him a harp and a crown: his body is given a triumphal burial, and his monument will be visited annually.

This conclusion – that might be termed 'pagan' – is pure classic tragedy. The audience, whether the late reader by the light of his solitary lamp, or half the local population leaning forward in the warm sunshine, turns away, feeling that it shares with the Chorus 'true experience from this great event', the *cartharsis*, or purification of the emotions (according to Aristotle) by pity and terror aroused by what they have witnessed. They emerge 'calm of mind, all passion spent'.

Plot and structure

The plot is classical in its simplicity and is well summarized by Milton himself in The Argument, with one revealing deficiency: Dalila and Harapha are not referred to by name, but only as 'other persons'. In the Preface Milton explains that as the poem is not intended for stage presentation he has omitted the usual division into acts and scenes, while indicating that it does not extend beyond the equivalent of five acts, the structure taken by Renaissance playwrights from the ancients and further divided into scenes. However, by comparison with a typical Greek tragedy – the *Bacchae* of Euripides (translated by Gilbert Murray) provides a useful example – the characteristic division into 'episodes' (in dialogue) and 'stasima' (choral hymns) can be superimposed on our text:

Structure according to the Greek pattern:

1	Prologue	Monologue by Samson, after his guide has left him.
115	Parados	Entrance of Chorus: the pitiable state of the former champion.
176	Episode 1	Dialogue: Samson and Chorus.
293	Stasimon	(Chorus in position): God's will must not be questioned.
326	Episode 2	Dialogue: Samson, Manoa and Chorus.
606		Monologue by Samson: in his misery he prays for death.
652	Stasimon	Unfair punishment of patriots.
710	Episode 3	Dialogue: Samson, Dalila and Chorus.
1010	Stasimon	Feminine unreliability, hence masculine rule.
1061	Episode 4	Dialogue: Samson, Harapha and Chorus.
1268	Stasimon	Patience, as well as might, has power to deliver.
1297	Episode 5	Dialogue: Samson, Officer and Chorus.
1427	Stasimon	(Chorus alone after Samson's departure): call to Samson's angel and his former spirit to aid him.
1441	Exodus	Dialogue: Manoa, Chorus and Messenger.
		Monologue by Messenger (the 'catastrophe').
		Final Chorus: Mission accomplished.
		1st Semi-chorus: The fate of the Philistines.
		2nd Semi-chorus: The prowess of Samson.
		Monologue by Manoa: A monument to the Victor.
		Epilogue by Chorus: Calm at the close.

The Unities

The three 'unities' of Time, Place and Action were theoretical principles based, by certain critics from the Renaissance onwards, on Greek drama; such unity as the Greeks practised, however, was arrived at by experience in their own theatres, and not formulated in strict rules. On their small stages, before huge audiences in the open air, it was convenient to limit events to those happening on the same day, at the same place (no scene-shifting), and without a complicating sub-plot. Such conditions also explain masks to represent sad or merry moods and thick-soled boots to raise the principal actors above the Chorus.

In *Samson Agonistes* Milton has observed the three unities: (1) a one-day holiday laid on by his captors; (2) his resting place outside the prison and away from the crowds is suited to closely argued dialogue, yet near enough to hear the theatre collapse; (3) the action consists of a series of confrontations in the reproaches of a doting father, the attempted seductions of a faithless 'wife', the cowardly taunts of a rival champion, the abrupt commands of the Officer backed by threats. All lead to the resolution, which a feeling of renewed strength gives him, to use any opportunity offered to one who cannot see. He has a presentiment of some great exploit – the imaginary audience know the outcome in advance. Nevertheless, when the crash comes, i.e. the noise off-stage and the arrival of the terrified but by no means tongue-tied Messenger, the tragic awe is overwhelming. The mental picture is one of devastation on a 'nuclear' scale, a slaughter of the hated foes which would be a subject for rejoicing did it not involve the hero's death in the hour of victory.

This, then, is the tragedy: the death of the hero, a character of outstanding qualities but with a fatal weakness that leads him to folly, defeat and ultimate death. With Samson it was a case of betraying to a woman the secret of his supernatural strength and succumbing to her amorous caresses in a slumber during which his hair was treacherously shorn. The blinding and – even worse – the captive slavery that swiftly followed, are the tragic consequences of his fatal flaw. All this antedates the opening of the drama. The tragedy is with us throughout: in almost continuous argument; self-blame and blaming others; questioning God's will and His heartless treatment of His servants; woman's erring tongue and easy yielding to pressure; and victories denied by the hero's blindness.

Action is practically limited to entrances and exits and the utterance of threats. There is, nevertheless, the continuous development that transforms Samson from a dejected slave to a death-dealing warrior. It begins with the announcement of the Dagon festival, which is an insult to the Hebrew God. This Samson sees as a challenge that God will not overlook, and his confidence begins to return. The episodes form a true climax, a series of steps to the final catastrophe: Manoa's offer of a quiet corner for a ransomed prisoner; Dalila's familiar blandishments and the attempt to touch his hand; Harapha's cowardly sneers, which stir Samson's fighting instincts; the Officer's curt commands. All are successive goads to action.

A fatal mistake is now made by the other side. They wish to exult over their captive giant in public, being entertained as by a performing bear of huge proportions and watching from an architectural masterpiece with a roof (or gallery?) constructed to rest on a pair of centrally placed pillars! Not a pagan Fate, but God's will, working mysteriously through the wiles of a wanton woman, creates greater havoc than all the champion's previous exploits put together. The 'tragic' end is no longer the traditional 'waste' of fine human material, but a threefold and instantaneous success. The enemies against whom he was originally sent have been effectively crushed; the honour of Samson, his family and his tribe has been redeemed, and his own miserable existence brought to an end.

As the reader lays down the script of this 17th century 'spectacular' he can feel the silence as the soft-footed Chorus flit across the sand of the orchestra to the exit – the silence up there in the curved seats rising tier above tier to meet the blue Mediterranean sky.

Characters

Samson

This hero is the central character throughout the play. From his first appearance to his departure for the theatre he is either arguing or listening to the argument of others; even out of sight he is the subject of hopes and speculations, which turn to lamentation or admiration. Milton's title follows Greek example, like *Oedipus Rex*. The 'agon' was an assembly of various states for competition in athletics and the arts (rather like the Welsh *eisteddfod*). 'Agonistes' meant a competitor, an actor, or (as in the case of Samson) a champion. Samson emerged from no competition, for he had been divinely selected to champion the oppressed Israelites. His earlier feats, indeed, took the form of large-scale brawls, in which he involved himself through his love affairs. He was, however, aware of a mission assigned to him from birth, and justifiably resented the compromising attitude of the leaders of his nation when his miraculous strength was at their service. The play is about Samson's fate, not as a competitor but as a national champion and divine instrument.

Samson qualifies for the role of tragic hero in the two main respects: his sheer physical strength is not only an asset to his people, it measures up to the scale of those Greek dramas in which the characters are gods with superhuman powers. His fatal flaw is a glaring one, not one incidental slip but a repeated invitation to betrayal until, despite successive warnings, he yields to feminine importunity and blurts out his secret for the sake of peace and quiet. Or was it? Would a present-day psychologist detect an obsessive desire to find a woman he could both love and trust?

Apart from his addiction to the other sex, he has admirable qualities. He respects his father for the good upbringing he gave him and for his tactful handling of his waywardness; for his pride in family and his endeavours to ransom him. Yet, better to die than linger on as a useless hulk by the domestic fire. His outspoken remarks to Dalila, in reply to a cleverly argued case, are an eloquent warning against falling an easy victim to feminine wiles. He will give her no more pardon for her outrageous betrayal than he gives himself for proving such a failure as a champion. He exposes the hollowness of Harapha's boasting by a direct challenge, and replies to his insults with careful argument. Then, in his turn, he boasts what he will do with this 'tongue-doughty giant' if he can lay hands on him.

From his own experience Milton was able to give real emotional depth to this old biblical story. We are shown the progression from utter dejection ('I shall shortly be with them that rest') to confident resolution ('This day will be remarkable in my life'). In what was to Milton a national disaster (when monarchy, prelacy and profligacy had the upper hand; when all he had worked for, and for which he had sacrificed his sight, was overthrown), he wrought for himself an imaginary triumphal slaughter of the 'Philistines'. Perhaps he hoped that the crash in Gaza would reverberate in the minds of Restoration readers. There is one easily overlooked difference between Milton and his hero. Milton's eyesight was extinguished without any apparent blemish (see the second sonnet to Skinner); Samson would have been left with empty sockets, to which no kind of vision could have returned. As 'foreign secretary' Milton was keenly aware of the importance of state secrets. In his view, Samson's revelation of the secret of his strength, so vital to national defence, was more serious than his liaison with a beautiful foreign agent. It was for this that he forfeited God's favour.

Manoa

Manoa and the Chorus are on the side of Samson: Dalila, Harapha and the Officers are Philistines. Manoa, conspicuous on this classical stage with his 'locks white as down', makes two entrances that frame the central action of the play: he departs to pursue his negotiations for a ransom behind the scenes; and he returns in time to share with the Chorus the shock and the triumph of the catastrophe.

Samson's erratic career is reflected in the utterances of his father, a worthy old man, absorbed in his son's fate, and a tireless negotiator with a succession of hostile foreigners. While the Chorus give expression to national feelings, Manoa is the archetypal father of the son from whom so much is expected – and this son one whose birth was, as we are repeatedly reminded, twice announced by an angel to a barren woman. In the Bible narrative we see the Manoa of our play asking questions. What are the instructions for the child's upbringing? What will the Messenger have to eat? What is his name? Manoa then proceeds with the ritual offering on an altar, in the flame from which the angel ascends heavenwards. The father's pride in a son dedicated as a Nazarite (whose hair must never be cut) with a mission to *begin* to liberate the Israelites from Philistine oppression, is given a shock by the young giant's interest in foreign women. However, after initial disapproval, he consents to appear at the wedding of the woman of Timnath.

Now Manoa's last hope is for his son to be freed from the degradation of prison by ransom (even if it costs him his entire inheritance) and brought home to be looked after. This is the basis for much of the dramatic irony that abounds in this play; his 'timely care' as a father is balanced against God's plan to bring colossal disaster on the national foe. In his first appearance he is tempted to reproach the God of his people with over-punishment, as well as mildly rebuking Samson for the disgrace of the feast about to be held for Dagon. But what weighs with him most is his own canvassing of Philistine leaders who, he believes, will agree that Samson is no longer a threat, and that he has been punished enough. He then has to dissuade Samson from a self-inflicted penalty and get him to consent to return to his own country, his family hearth and the worship of God – better bedridden than grinding alien corn. Further, as one who has spoken to an angel, Manoa contemplates a possible miracle, the restoration of sight to correspond with restored strength.

Rather than join the spectators at the festival, he returns to inform the Chorus of his partly successful efforts to arrange for the ransom. His account is first interrupted by the shout that greets Samson's appearance in the arena. Shortly after, when he is picturing his son at home, nursing his strength for some exploit, the crash everyone in the audience has been expecting so startles him that, when Chorus takes up his own suggestion of restored vision, he doubts such a miracle. Ever a man for facts, it is he who questions the Messenger, reluctant conveyor of the worst possible news.

His first reaction is the ironical comment that death has paid the ransom he was offering. Then he asks for details of the horrific event before he proceeds to mourn, and there follows a long uninterrupted account succeeded by a long celebration by the Chorus, chanted in the shorter lyric metre. All this while Manoa observes the traditional Hebrew silence. At length, recalling his companions from their poetical tribute, he introduces a businesslike, even stoic note: 'no time for lamentation now', or more simply, 'Nothing is here for tears.' After all, Samson has proved true to himself, brought disaster on his enemies and finally found favour with God. Manoa issues practical instructions for the funeral and the erection of a national monument in the family burial ground. The only cause for tears is briefly dismissed as a mistaken marriage, leading to blindness and imprisonment.

This is spoken like a true stoic, for Manoa has lost all that matters in his life. His way with the enemy was patient, persevering supplication backed by a bribe. Samson's way, apparently in tune with the Infinite, was colossal material vengeance: immediate and totally sacrificial.

Dalila

Next to himself, Samson's worst enemy is his wife (or concubine, or harlot: the status varies from speech to speech but is largely irrelevant). Dalila has not been the only woman to betray Samson but she is the one who succeeds, by sheer persistence and bravado, in extracting the true secret of his strength; she acts upon this, arranging the ambush by his enemies. In the biblical account this is as far as it goes. The Book of Judges is more concerned with the damage inflicted on the Philistines than with the motives of a heatheness who was merely a base instrument.

It is more usual for husband and wife to be at odds in comedy. The familiar infidelities rarely involve treason, death and national disaster. And in tragedy there are usually redeeming features in the main characters, be they Macbeth and his deadly partner or the fated heroes of Greek drama. Dalila is not only deceitful but utterly mercenary and shameless. To this nucleus of feminine wickedness Milton adds a show of repentance, a reliance on personal charms, and a subtle knowledge of her husband's forgiving ways.

A comparison with that other, more celebrated, example of feminine faithlessness, the mistress of the Garden of Eden and the direct agent in the loss of that Paradise, is natural. Eve is the tempted, not the tempter. She is Adam's devoted wife, flesh of his flesh, not a seducer from a foreign race. When she disobeys, her husband joins her (in Milton's version) out of love and the wish not to lose her. Dalila, as we are reminded by Samson himself, first captured him by her physical attraction, enslaved him with her embraces and then, heavily bribed by Philistine gold, got his 'secret' through persistent prayers and entreaties – then arranged his betrayal.

Three times Samson gave Dalila false information: seven 'green withs' [i.e. new ropes] and his seven locks woven into a web; three times she concealed men in her room ready to seize him, and three times he reduced her to ridicule. This was the most extraordinary betrayal of all time. Three times warned of this woman's treachery, brazenly repeated with each new request, the intended victim gave away the real secret. Not even the most tongue-battered husband, worn out by sheer importunity and exhausted by lack of sleep, would have been so stupid. On Dalila's fate after her 'patriotic' act, the Bible is silent.

It is this woman who appears before her blinded lover in what must seem a last brazen act of seduction. Is her elaborate dressing-up out of force of habit or to impress beholders with her improved social position? Samson is as blind to her arguments as he is unable to see all these feminine accessories. Her self-justification, with all its recollections of their past relationship, serves as a further stage in goading him into the spirit of terrible revenge. She pleads her case in speeches of some plausibility. Are all her utterances false? Samson thinks so, and by the time she leaves he is in a mind to strike her. She leaves him with all the fury of a woman scorned, gloating over the future fame her deed will bring her.

Harapha

Manoa brought a reminder of family disgrace, Dalila a reminder of his womanizing weakness. Harapha, a stranger whose face he has never seen, brings Samson a reminder of missed opportunities. This really gigantic Parisee represents the work for which Samson had been selected, the sphere of a national champion. It is probably this galling thought that leads Samson to reiterate his challenge so many times. He cannot see how powerfully built Harapha is, but he is eager to try his strength against the giant. Samson is now a very different character from the dejected figure at the opening of the play. The thought of this Philistine's bulk causes him to flex his muscles, half-consciously preparing himself for the vaster task of rending stones and mortar; he even seems to think in terms of demolition: 'And with one buffet lay thy structure low.' Perhaps Samson has detected in Harapha's voice the mere boaster who has so far managed to keep out of his way. After the pent-up emotions of the two previous visits there is welcome comic relief in Harapha's series of evasions.

Loudly voicing his regret that chance and blindness have robbed him of the opportunity of putting the Hebrew in his place, he is met with an immediate challenge to test his strength in a physical grapple. When he scorns a fight with a man blind *and* unwashed, he is given specific conditions: an oaken staff against his complete outfit of armour. He who came to scorn is now treated with scorn. Accusing Samson of relying on magic, he is challenged as Dagon's champion to meet God's. Harapha sarcastically points out that God has left his champion in the lurch, and goes on to describe Samson as murderer, rebel and robber. When these charges are refuted, he falls back on his first disdain to join in combat with a convicted slave, and departs uttering threats of what others will inflict on Samson.

Chorus

The Chorus, consisting of a group of fellow-tribesmen, are present throughout the play, thus reinforcing the unity of action. Their ideas and feelings are expressed by a single spokesman until the end, where there is division into two semi-choruses, each with its spokesman. The classic chorus has a double function of which Milton makes full use: it serves as the eyes of the hero, describing to him the arrival and departure of the other characters; and it gives tongue to the emotions of the spectators, real or imaginary.

The private reader, indeed, can see no more of the comings and goings than a blind man, unless he is informed and prepared for the ensuing dialogue. This the Chorus does effectively, breaking off from the high lyrical utterance of each stasimon to portray in appropriate fashion – deep pity, biting caricature or mere speculation – the approaching or receding figure. The stasima are mainly reflections on what the Chorus sees and hears, sympathizing with the hero and wondering about his fate. It wonders, too, what on earth led him to neglect Hebrew women for foreigners.

Minor characters

The *Officer* is suitably abrupt and officious, though not without courtesy and some sympathy. The *Guide* is typical of 'silent', i.e. non-speaking, characters in Greek drama. He disappears in line 11 and is not heard of again until line 1630 in the Messenger's account (if, indeed, he is the same), when Samson requests him to lead him to lean against the pillars. The *Messenger* is also Greek in the length of the report he gives to the end of Samson. He is, of course, no bearer of a message but witness of something that has necessarily taken place offstage. (In the *Bacchae* of Euripides the Messenger gives *two* long reports on the behaviour of those wild women, the Bacchantes – see the section on *The classical element*.)

Later style

Between the early lyrics and the dialogue of *Samson Agonistes* there intervened the two most important events in Milton's life: the publication of *Paradise Lost* in all its majesty of elaborately wrought diction; and the 'universal blank' (*Paradise Lost* 3,48) which cut him off from direct contact with the printed page. The two events now seem inseparable: blindness without the epic would have meant relative obscurity; the epic without loss of sight might well have fallen short of the superhuman scale on which it took shape in the mind of the poet, whose vision was no longer focused on the every-day objects of domestic surroundings and neighbourhood walks, but turned inwards. In his blindness his imagination more readily adapted itself to the vastness of space; the movement of great hosts; the massive conflict of aerial armies; bottomless abysses; marathon journeys; and a primeval landscape devoid of human habitation.

From this universe, in which God's plan for mankind is temporarily thwarted, we come down to the world of one man wrestling with his fate as God's failed champion. From the timeless manoeuvres in the sky and the leisurely lapse of cloudless days in Eden we shrink to the last few hours in Samson's life – with all the urgency of crisis, the emotional tension of humiliation upon humiliation – until all is brought to a conclusion by a holocaust. In *Samson Agonistes* Milton finds himself.

In *Comus*, *Paradise Lost*, *Paradise Regained* and *Samson Agonistes* Milton is the champion of blank verse; his sense of rhythm and his ear for a musical phrase enabled his verse to compete on a level with the best of heroic (rhyming) couplets and stanzas. The youthful exuberance of his earlier blank verse gives place in *Paradise Lost* to the disciplined metre of a lengthy poem; at the same time skilful manipulation of sound effects and variation of the *caesura* (a break between words in a *metrical foot*) avoided monotony. In *Samson Agonistes* the redundant syllable in *Comus* reappears, but as an aid to easier dialogue (as in Shakespeare's later plays); and in the course of sometimes heated arguments there are lapses into banality.

The figures of speech in *Samson* are mostly different from those in *Comus*: instead of picturesque epithets, sound-effects and personified abstractions, there are tricks with word order, devices for emphasis and, most noticeable, repetition throughout in varying forms of what is called 'tautology'. They all endeavour to impress or persuade. There is passionate emotion in such examples of *chiasmus* (inversion, in a second phrase, of the order of words used in the first phrase) as 'O impotence of mind, in body strong' and 'Scarce half I seem to live, dead more than half.'

From the same opening soliloquy comes the famous repetition: 'O dark, dark, dark, amid the blaze of noon,/Irrecoverably dark' and tautology with a purpose in 'Myself my sepulchre, a moving grave', which follows closely an oxymoron, 'a living death'. Tautology again in 'Inferior to the vilest ... the vilest here excel me.' In the same passage, between lines 70 and 100, the key word 'light' is used eight times, in an agony of regret at the loss of it. The last two actually form an identical rhyme. 'Weakness' is used three times in three lines in lines 829–31.

Repetition for emphasis: 'Sole author I, sole cause/Spare that proposal, Father, spare the trouble/Of that solicitation/My race of glory run, and race of shame'.

Also contrast: '... self-displeased/For self-offence, more than for God offended'.

In lines 491–9 repetition in the form of a climax: 'Secrets of men, the secrets of a friend/... His holy secret.'

There is the same use of echo in bringing together allied words: 'to oppress Israel's oppressors/heroicly hath finished/A life heroic'. There is a striking example in lines 270–1 of repetition in which epithets are added in the second line to Bondage and Liberty, and this is arranged as a *chiasmus*. Lines 652–9 contain an elaborate *chiasmus*, the first three lines being expanded in the five lines of the second part. The verse of *Comus* might be described as a richly coloured tapestry; that of *Samson Agonistes* as resembling a full-sized statue engaged in a struggle.

Milton's adherence to blank verse – in an age of increasingly conventional couplets – for the writing of a drama on a Greek model isolated in form and spirit from the contemporary stage, as well as his reversion to the Italian-type sonnet after the success of the Elizabethan – all are a reflection of that early stubbornness of mind that he manifested at the university – not to mention the republican pamphlet he published on the very eve of the Restoration! This is what Wordsworth was thinking of when he wrote that Milton 'dwelt apart'.

From Spenser he probably acquired a liking for the other-worldly effect of archaisms – he would have had little sympathy for modernist versions of prayer-book language! To most people Milton's poems, in so far as they are aware of them, are nearly as incomprehensible as an unknown tongue. Perhaps it takes a scholar, or aspiring scholar, to appreciate him fully. Thomas Gray, buried almost exactly a century later in nearby Stoke Poges, coined an imperishable phrase for an imagined uneducated villager lying in his churchyard: 'Some mute inglorious Milton here may rest.' Such a one would have lacked the advantages that Milton put to such good purpose.

The biblical element

The well-known story of Samson (the name means 'like the sun') is told in chapters 13–16 of the Book of Judges. It is now regarded as a version of an old folk-take (or several tales rolled into one) made by a chronicler who was compiling a series of heroic achievements against enemy nations by various 'judges' (i.e. leaders or dictators) who, from time to time, kept the Hebrew tribes together. Because of his gigantic personal performances Samson was given the title of Judge, and the conventional period of twenty years' rule. These were turbulent times. Not only were there frequent conflicts with various nations, but the Israelites themselves were constantly forsaking their own religion; 'doing evil in the sight of the Lord'; adopting foreign rites or marrying into alien races; then being punished by national disaster and saved by a chosen leader. This process – sin, oppression, salvation – was repeated at intervals.

In fact, Samson's heroic death did not put an end to Philistine domination. This people, a mysterious one from overseas, with their five cities (Ascalon, Ashdod, Ekron, Gath and Gaza), were bitter enemies until Hebrew kings were appointed and David 'smote' them. At one point they captured the Ark in Shiloh, but when they placed it in the temple of their god Dagon, the latter was found flat on its face next morning. Of the twelve tribes of Israel, Dan, to which Samson belonged, was one of the smallest and adjoined the Philistines on the north.

Milton dramatized the last day of Samson's life. Other incidents, such as the riddle of the strong and the sweet (a very ancient one), the ass's jaw-bone, and the successive bindings are introduced in speeches that look backwards, comparing past with present. The most significant addition by Milton was Samson's consciousness of disloyalty to God and of failure in his great mission; also, the complaint by the Chorus that God used His servants harshly when they failed, without consideration for previous services rendered. There was an ancient belief that strength corresponded to the length of one's hair, and the Nazarites went unshaven, but there was nothing of the religious association given it by Milton. In the Bible Samson simply prayed for strength to be revenged upon the Philistines for putting out his eyes. All his agony of mind and bitter remorse are the poet's invention.

At those times the law was not so strict about marriages with women of other nations; also, concubinage was an accepted inferior form of marriage. In the Bible Dalila is not referred to as Samson's wife, unlike the woman from Timnath whom he chose as wife and who was reluctantly recognized by his father. Milton makes him speak of her first as a 'deceitful concubine', but when she appears it is 'My wife, my traitress'.

There are a number of anachronisms, the most striking of which is the list of performers at Dagon's feast which reads like a day at St Bartholomew's Fair in London: 'Have they not sword-players, and every sort/Of gymnic artists, wrestlers, riders, runners,/Jugglers and dancers, antics, mummers, mimics?'

i.e. not chronologically speaking!

Summaries and textual notes

Lines 1–114

Samson is led to his favourite bank and left to enjoy the fresh air and soliloquize: his spoken words serve both to express the tumult of his own emotions and to inform (or remind) the audience of the facts of his situation. In thus anticipating the various themes of the play about to be unfolded – his special upbringing, his surrender to female blandishments, his humiliation, and with particular emphasis in this prologue the loss of his eyes – this opening speech resembles the overture to an opera. The contrast is between then and now.

Samson asks why this should happen to one whose high birth was foretold to his parents and who was given special training; why this divinely ordained strength should, instead of liberating Israel, be put to work with slaves. He answers the question by taking all the blame – the flesh was strong but the will was weak; strength uncontrolled by wisdom soon leads to disaster. God's hidden purpose must not be questioned, but blindness is hard to bear. The sound of footsteps warns him of an approaching group.

dark steps The epithet is transferred from the unseeing eyes to the stumbling footsteps. *Hypallage* (a transferred epithet; see p.21 is frequent in this work. There is also *metonymy* (substitution of an *attribute* for the person or thing it is linked to, e.g. 'crown' for 'king') in the 'guiding hand'.

else At other times.

draught Air drawn into the lungs.

day-spring Dawn.

leave me The guide is an instance of the 'silent' characters of Greek plays. Cf. Dalila's 'damsel train behind', who are not even addressed.

Sea-Idol Dagon, the Philistine god, was half man, half fish.

no sooner found alone i.e. when they come upon me by myself.

Twice by an Angel See Judges, 13, especially verses 5 and 20.

separate to God Set apart for service to God. A Nazarite 'separated' himself from indulgences.

Gaza One of the five chief Philistine cities, close to the Mediterranean Sea.

highest dispensation The divine ordering of things.

extinct Extinguished (today means 'dead').

first created Beam Light was the first thing made by God. A 'beam', when used to mean 'ray', has the suggestion of strength and reassurance.

great Word i.e. the order expressed in the next line (Genesis, 1,3). Cf. John, 1,1: 'In the beginning was the Word.'

bereaved thy prime decree Robbed of what you first ordered to come into existence.

silent A Latin use (*luna silens*) meaning 'inactive moon', and so not shining. There is poetic licence in confusing the two senses.

vacant interlunar cave This well-known phrase invites various interpretations: How can the cave be vacant when the moon is in it? If it is 'interlunar' it must lie between the two moons, the old and the new, so splitting the moon as a personified being.

light is in the Soul Here again two senses are blended, the light of understanding and the light of the eyes.

all in every part Equally diffused all over, as in line 96.

obvious Readily met with. The Latin *obviam* literally meant 'lying in the road'; from this our modern word is derived.

as feeling As feeling (sensation) is.

half dead A repetition of line 79, further paraphrased in lines 101 and 103.

privilege A special right (ironical) conferred by virtue of being dead and buried.

obnoxious Exposed (to something harmful). The opposite of 'exempt' in line 103.

joint pace This suggests the drilled movement of a chorus, rather than the broken step of a band of friends.

feet steering *Metonymy*.

115–175

The newcomers, fellow-tribesmen from Dan, shocked at the transformation of their hero, pause at a distance. Contrasting the dejected figure on the bank with the former warrior performing miracles against whole armies, they echo, in a similar lyrical metre, Samson's utterances on the double imprisonment of shackles and sightlessness. They add the reflection that the fall of great ones is more catastrophic than that of the less distinguished, whatever their social position.

at random In heedless fashion (without control).

diffused Sprawling.

languish'd Drooping.

habit Clothes.

tore the Lion See Judges, 14,5–6.

Cuirass Breast-plate.

Chalybean-temper'd Brought to the right state of hardness and elasticity in the manner of the Chalybes, a race of Asia Minor once famous for their manufactures from the abundant iron of their country.

frock of mail Tunic of chain-mail, body-armour formed of interlaced rings.

Adamantean Proof i.e. tested for extreme hardness. Adamant was a general term for the hardest stone or metal, e.g. diamond (a derivative of this word) or steel.

insupportably Irresistibly.

his foot i.e. Samson's.

Spurn'd Kicked, trampled upon. It now has the meaning of 'scorn' in the previous line.

Ascalonite Citizen of Ascalon, another of the five Philistine cities.

Lion ramp Lion-like spring.

fore-skins Philistines (uncircumcised).

Ramath-lechi The name given by Samson to the battlefield, traditionally rendered as 'the lifting-up of the ass's jaw-bone'. It could also mean a high rock looking like a jaw-bone and giving rise to this incredible exploit (though scarcely more incredible than that of the following lines).

Assa Another name for Gaza (both mean 'strong').

Hebron Ancient and sacred city some forty miles from Gaza, where the giant race of the Anakim used to live.

No journey No small distance, like the three-quarters of a mile permitted on the Hebrew day of rest.

Like whom ... Heav'n Like Atlas. (See *The classical element*.)

the Gentiles feign The Greeks imagine. An anachronism, since they lived centuries after Samson.

Inseparably dark i.e. with no gleam of light from which to distinguish the darkness.

The Dungeon of thyself The Chorus's parallel to 'a moving grave', line 102.

Men enjoying sight i.e. philosophers who think of the body as a prison in which the soul languishes.

The rarer ... By how much Your example is made more unusual in proportion to the extent to which ...

I reckon This *Chorus* is throughout the spokesman for the group.

the sphere of fortune Strictly the wheel of Fortune, a goddess widely worshipped in classical times and sometimes represented with a wheel in her hands to signify the changing turns in individual careers.

thee The second object of 'reckon in high estate'.

176–292

The Chorus offer words of comfort, which are received gratefully as coming from true friends. Samson wonders if he, the ex-champion, is now universally mocked; he wonders also why God did not make his wisdom as great as his strength. Taxed with associating with Philistine women he explains that they were to be the means by which he was to deliver Israel; it was his own weakness that led to failure. But more to blame for the continued oppression were the leaders of Judah, who, preferring peace to liberation, held back from joining in the attack and even handed him over bound to their enemies. The Chorus recall similar treacherous attitudes towards Gideon and Jephtha.

grief Cause of grief.

***Eshtaol* and *Zora's* fruitful Vale** These two places are mentioned in connection with Samson's youth (Judges, 13,25), and burial (Judges, 16,31).

swage Assuage, relieve the pain of.

who friends ... Superscription Who (seen as coins) merely have *friends* inscribed on them (speaking of the majority).

withdraw their head A vivid expression for absenting themselves.

nothing more than mean Barely average.

transverse In a direction diverging from the right course (a nautical reference back to the metaphor of a vessel in line 199).

pretend they ne'er so wise However much they claim to be wiser (than that).

besides i.e. besides the burden of self-criticism.

thine own Tribe Dan.

Timna Properly Timnath, a Philistine city (see Judges, 14,1).

not my parents i.e. my parents were displeased. Omissions complicate this sentence.

by occasion hence By some opportunity in this way.

Sorec See Judges, 16,4.

Israel **still serves** i.e. the whole nation is subject to the enemy.

ambition Canvassing (for favourable opinions). The literal meaning.

Etham See Judges, 15,8.

was retired Had withdrawn.

harass The laying waste (obselete as a noun).

on some conditions Namely, that they themselves would not attack him when bound.

were threads ... flame 'Became as flax that was burnt with fire' (Judges, 15,14).

a trivial weapon i.e. the jaw-bone of an ass.

Succoth ... Penuel Two cities that refused to provision Gideon's army during his pursuit of the Midianites (Madian in the next line).

Ephraim A large Israelite tribe named after a son of Joseph. For their quarrel with Jephtha, see Judges, 1–7.

Had dealt Would have dealt.

by argument i.e. in a long letter to the King of the Ammonites. See Judges, 11,12–27.

Shibboleth The Ephraimites were betrayed by their mispronunciation of this word 'Sibboleth' and were slain in huge numbers at the river crossing.

such examples i.e. of men betrayed by others of the same nation.

293–325

The Chorus becomes involved in some tricky theology. God's methods are open to reasonable explanation, yet, apart from the folly of atheism, there are many of the faithful who criticize His apparent injustices; whereas He is above human law. He has some purpose in leading Samson to break the taboo on foreign marriages (which were 'unclean' to the Hebrews).

who think not God at all i.e. the Atheists.

obscure In the darkness.

School i.e. a body of thinkers of the same mind.

the heart of the Fool i.e. the only 'school' of this kind, in which the fool himself is the leading scholar.

th' interminable The Infinite (God). (Nowadays used of something lasting too long.)

National obstriction Prohibition binding on the nation as a whole, such as a mixed marriage.

who never wanted ... cause Who always had the power, as well as a pretext, supplied by the infidel nations themselves.

Nazarite One who took vows (sometimes for life) of purity and abstention from wine; and who did not cut his hair.

Unclean, unchaste This emphatic line distinguishes between Dalila's 'uncleanness' as a Gentile and the 'unchastity' of her behaviour after her marriage (it should be noted that no marriage is mentioned in the biblical account).

aver May state.

verdit Older form of 'verdict', as 'quits' is of 'acquits'.

326–651

Three visitors rouse, in different ways, Samson's antagonistic spirit accompanying his returning physical strength. The first is his aged father, Manoa, who can hardly recognize his once invincible son in the dejected figure before him. He is driven to bewail the gift of so distinguished a child and to protest that the punishment was excessive for one who had, after all, done great service as a champion.

Samson takes on himself the entire blame. He has given away God's secret to a foreign woman in spite of an earlier betrayal by her predecessor, and of previous attempts by Dalila herself. He should have resisted her passionate importunities, but his fondness for women – a 'slavery' worse than his present condition – made him yield.

Manoa agrees that his son's succumbing to temptation was a sin that he is now expiating to the full; a worse disgrace is the triumph their enemies are about to hold (with sacrifices to Dagon) in celebration of their victory.

Samson accepts the blame also for this dishonour to God and consequent discouragement to the Israelites. His only hope is that Dagon, having challenged God, will meet with his deserts.

When Manoa tells him about the approaches he is making to the Philistines for a ransom, Samson rejects what would be a lingering humiliation and is determined to suffer to the utmost. Manoa pleads with him to leave punishment to God, instead of inflicting it on himself. Samson asks what life can hold for him, once so proud of his strength, now that infatuation has deprived him of it.

When the Chorus, in what seems a digression in praise of abstinence from strong drink, finds something to praise in his conduct, Samson retorts that resistance to one temptation is useless without resistance to all· the remainder of his life can only be miserable existence.

Manoa finally upbraids him for preferring to put his newly reviving strength at the service of the Philistines; at home he might even have his sight restored. He leaves the despairing Samson to pursue his negotiations.

Samson now bewails the fact that torment can be spiritual as well as physical. His sorrows fester like a disease and plague him like insects. He welcomes death. This lyrical outburst contrasts once more his heroic past with his wretched present, and he prays to be allowed to die.

careful Full of care, woe-begone.
advise/Forthwith Bethink yourself at once.
uncouth i.e. strange (because unfamiliar).
old respect Regard for Samson as he was. Subject of 'hath informed'.
inform'd Directed.
cast back Handicapped (by deterioration).
signal i.e. conspicuous.
Duell'd their Armies Fought them as if he were meeting a single adversary.
Graces Divine favours.
draw a Scorpion's tail behind i.e. sting like a scorpion.
thrall Slave.
Appoint not heav'nly disposition Do not criticize God's plan.
profaned Desecrated.
Canaanite Dalila was a Philistine, one of a people who invaded and occupied the coastal area of Canaan.
The secret The answer to his riddle of the lion and the honey. See Judges, 14,5–18.
faithless Heathen. Perhaps word-play on her disloyalty to him. (Cf. line 388.)
Nuptial Wedded.
vitiated Corrupted.

by the scent conceived ... against me i.e. the mere offer of money was sufficient to create in her, instead of a child, treachery towards me.

summ'd Concentrated.

must'ring Assembling in readiness for action. Followed by 'parleys', 'assaults', 'batteries' and 'storm', it forms an extended metaphor.

effeminacy Fondness for women.

infest Attack persistently (now used of vermin and insects.)

state not Do not dispute.

rigid score Clearly marked debt (from the notches on a tally stick).

Them out of thine i.e. (delivered) the Philistines out of thy hands.

the most with shame The shamefullest.

obloquy Abuse.

oped the mouths Given (them) the opportunity to boast.

diffidence of Lack of confidence in.

propense Inclined. The noun 'propensity' is used today.

enter lists Compete. From the 'lists', the space for tilting in tournaments.

confusion Panic-stricken disorder. It is derived from 'confound' and is much stronger here than its modern use.

blank Disconcert. Another form of 'blanch', to turn something white.

defer ... vindicate Delay in upholding.

made way Approached.

hainous Hateful (from Fr. *haine*).

fact i.e. action.

front Forehead (as in French).

Gentiles Greeks. Samson lived long before their day.

Parables Here means myths.

To their Abyss ... confined Imprisoned in Hades (Hell) and (subjected to) torments. (This is the classical sentence construction called 'zeugma'.)

act not in thy own affliction Do not apply the rod yourself.

high disposal God's providing.

penal forfeit Payment inflicted as punishment.

what offer'd means ... return thee Whatever means (of escape) may be made available – who knows but that God has already provided it for us – to bring you back.

sacred house Probably the Jewish Tabernacle.

beyond i.e. exceeding those of.

Sons of Anak See Deuteronomy, 9,2. Cf. line 148.

blazed Trumpeted. From a root-word meaning 'to blow'.

venereal trains Love stratagems.

hallow'd pledge i.e. his hair.

shore me Cut off from me.

Ruby Wine.

Crystalline Transparent as crystal, translucent.

Against the Eastern ray Towards the sunrise.

fiery rod Rays from the sun.

milky juice An extraordinary phrase, possibly transferring the sweetness of milk and the stimulus of the juice of the grape to water.

What boots it What use is it?

visitants i.e. callers at the house.

redundant Billowing like waves (literally, 'flowing').

Robustious to no purpose i.e. their luxuriance is now severed from strength (Cf. the next line).

craze Weaken.

draff of servile food Refuse fed to slaves.

oft-invocated Often appealed to. We now use 'invoked'.

annoy Do harm to; stronger than in the modern sense.

this strength ... remaining This marvellous strength still left. Does Manoa contemplate new feats by Samson with restored eyesight?

portend Foretell.

double darkness i.e. death.

genial spirits Natural faculties.

them that rest i.e. the dead.

humours black Moods of depression. Melancholy was thought to be caused by an excess of black bile, one of the four 'humours' in the body which influenced temperament; the other three were blood, water and yellow bile.

O that Expressing regret, not a wish. The varying length of line and the more irregular rhythm show an increase of passion.

exercise all his fierce accidents Put into operation all his (torment's) cruel devices (literally, symptoms).

on her purest spirits prey Attack the most sensitive faculties of the mind (personified as female). For 'spirits' cf. line 594.

void of corporal sense Lacking any physical sensation.

ferment and rage Verbs, as are also the three in line 621.

immedicable Incurable.

Mangle ... tenderest parts i.e. injure the most impressionable parts of my mind.

exulcerate Cause ulcers to break out.

Vernal Springtime (adjective).

Alp Strictly the upper pasture, but poetically and popularly the high mountain.

message Messenger.

twice descending The third reference to this special announcement of his birth.

nerve Strength (obsolete: the original meaning of Latin 'nervus' is muscle).

repeated Treated repeatedly as.

652–709

In spite of all that has been written about the virtues of patience under suffering, the actual sufferer finds little to soothe him in such philosophy; sole remedy is inner comfort from God. Yet what has Man, elect and endowed, done to deserve savage reversals of fortune unknown among angels above, animals below, and ordinary men? Cut off at the height of their powers the great fall lower even than the extent by which they rose, condemned by biased judges, hooted by the mob, betrayed and done to death, their very corpses treated with indignity. Unless they survive to a decrepit old age, afflicted with the diseases deserved only by worthless wastrels. There seems to be no distinction between the just and the unjust. All the Chorus can pray for is a peaceful end for Samson.

enroll'd Recorded.

chances incident to Misfortunes liable to befall.

Temper'st Modifies, adapts.

thy glory ... safety i.e. for God and Israel.

in part they effect i.e. their mission is only partly accomplished. The whole chorus is a generalization from Samson's case, though it has much confirmation in history. (Also autobiographical!)

remit ... obscured Send down to a life in hiding or lacking in recognition (as a magistrate commits a prisoner).

Unseemly falls in human eye Undeservedly humiliating downfalls in the view of all men.

Too grievous ... omission Too severe (a punishment) for doing something wrong or for doing nothing at all.

tribunals A reference to the trial of the Regicides after the Restoration and that of Sir Henry Vane (see Sonnet 13). Dead ones like Cromwell, Ireton and Bradshaw were disinterred and their bodies hanged publicly on the gallows.

crude Premature (from unripe fruit).

disordinate Leading a disorderly life.

causeless suff'ring ... days Unfairly suffering the same punishment as those guilty of disgraceful actions.

miserable To be pitied.

alike i.e. in their fate, but not in their character.

So In this manner.

Image Bodily representation.

minister Servant.

710–1009

The Chorus announces to Samson the arrival of Dalila, magnificently arrayed but in tears.

Dalila begins by declaring that, having wept copiously over her betrayal of him, wifely concern now urges her to see him once more and learn how she can make amends.

Samson immediately denounces this trick of professing repentance for wrongs done and promising better behaviour in the future; this is merely to try out her husband's patience and willingness to forgive in order to repeat the whole process, thus keeping him in perpetual misery.

Dalila next excuses her action as due to woman's weaknesses: curiosity and talkativeness. Samson, however, showed equal weakness himself in revealing his secret. A stronger motive – jealousy of his love – made her try to get him into her power; assured by the Philistines that they only wished to hold him prisoner, she expected to have him to herself.

Samson retorts that she is entitled to the same forgiveness that he gives himself! Weakness could be the plea of any criminal. How could her love (lust) hope to keep his by an act of betrayal?

Dalila denies that money influenced her; rather it was the appeal by the leaders of her nation to be a patriot and snare the nation's greatest foe. After lengthy consideration she sacrificed her private feeling to the public interest.

This is dismissed by Samson as hypocrisy. When she married him she left her people for his; their scheme to destroy him through her was contrary to the 'law of nations', and if this was an example of their gods' principles they were unfit to be gods at all.

Abandoning argument, Dalila begs for forgiveness and the chance to make amends by surrounding him with home comforts and tender nursing.

Samson is now too wary of her enticements to be caught again. Besides, if she betrayed him at the height of his powers how would she treat him now that he is helpless – and would she not report everything to her masters?

To her request to be allowed to touch his hand he replies by warning her that he might tear her to pieces. He dismisses her with a sarcastic wish that she enjoy her fame as the patriotic wife who sold her husband for gold.

Determined to have the last word, Dalila will no longer try to placate the implacable, receiving only insults in return. Fame is two-sided: if she is to become infamous in Israelite history, she will be commemorated in her own land. She is content with her lot.

When she is gone the Chorus ventures to hint at heartache in such a parting, only to be told firmly that lovers' quarrels often have a happy ending, but not treachery between wife and husband.

Tarsus The Greek city in Asia Minor where St Paul was born. Tarshish, a Phoenician settlement in Spain, would be more appropriate; it is frequently mentioned in the Old Testament.

Javan Javan, son of Japheth, youngest son of Noah, was the legendary ancestor of the Ionian Greeks. His sons, including Tarshish, divided the Isles of the Gentiles (i.e. the Aegean) among themselves.

Gadier Probably the Spanish port of Cadiz, spelt in the Greek way.

bravery Finery.

hold them play Play with them.

Amber scent Here probably ambergris, produced by the sperm whale and long used as perfume.

address'd Prepared (for speaking). Cf. line 731.

the fact i.e. my act of betrayal.

perverse event Adverse outcome.

estate State of health.

Hyaena This animal, whose name is a term of abuse, can imitate the human voice.

instructed Experienced (with lessons learned from previous actions).

publish them Repeat them in public.

For importunity ... for naught Because of my badgering you – which was nothing serious.

But I ... should not Stating the case against herself, and then answering it.

parle Parley, negotiate terms (either verb or noun).

That made for me That (proposal) was to my advantage.

widow'd bed Cf. modern 'grass-widow'.

unhazarded abroad Not running risks in your absences. This qualifies Samson, whereas 'Fearless' refers to 'myself'.

fond Foolish.

which Refers to 'pardon'.

Parricide Murderer of a father or near relative.

But Love constrained thee Introducing another of her arguments.

Knowing Refers to 'me' in the line above.

shame with shame i.e. shameful act with shameful lying.

determin'st weakness for no plea Decides that weakness cannot be accepted as a valid plea for the defence.

the priest Is Milton thinking of the Anglican parson rather than the Philistine temple priest?

Virtue ... so enjoining i.e. being instructed (as I believed) by virtue, truth and duty.

I thought I knew.

circling Roundabout.

Thou mine i.e. you were my subject and under my protection.

state Power.

violating the ends Offending against God's will for His chosen people.

Gods cannot be i.e. such cannot be true gods.

varnish'd colours Clever excuses.

For want of words ... breath Heavy sarcasm.

thy peals Cf. line 235.

Afford me place Allow me an opportunity.

Bear not too sensibly Suffer from not too acutely.

insist ... afflict Persist in inflicting.

care and chance Anxiety and accident.

grateful Pleasing.

accursed Under a spell.

trains Tricks. Cf. line 533.

gins Snares.

toils Nets.

Adder's wisdom This snake had a reputation for refusing to be charmed.

fence Screen.

slight Disdain.

insult Exult (unlike the modern meaning).

uxorious Used of a husband who dotes on his wife. (Latin: *uxor*: 'wife').

gloss upon Interpret.

censuring i.e. judging.

denounced Pronounced.

concernments Affairs.

the Circumcised i.e. the Israelites.

traduced Misrepresented.

Ecron … Gath These with Ascalon formed the five principal Philistine cities. Dalila is speaking in Gaza.

odours Incense.

in Mount *Ephraim* Where dwelt the prophetess Deborah, who sang the deed of Jael (Judges, 4,5).

Jael See Judges, 4,17–22.

inhospitable guile i.e. treachery towards a guest.

piety Faithfulness, especially to the nation.

whoever Oblique reference to Samson.

manifest Evident.

inward passion Inner suffering.

amorous remorse Pity inspired by (former) love.

1010–1060

The Chorus now pronounces the Miltonic solution to the problem of marriage. Since what moves a woman to love is a mystery; since the finest qualities in a man are no guarantee against her disloyalty; since her judgement and regard for others is not equal to her attractions; since the most charming bride may steer a marriage on to the rocks; and since a naturally good wife is a rarity, the highest course is to secure the victory of virtue over temptation. Therefore authority was bestowed from above on the man over the woman, not to be abrogated at any time, whatever the consequent tantrums.

inherit i.e. hold.

refer Seek to trace the origin of.

thy riddle See Judges 14,5–18. Also cf. lines 382–7.

in one … seven Samson challenged the young men to find the answer in seven days.

Paranymph Best man (at his wedding). This term was also used for a bridesmaid.

both i.e. she of Timna, and Dalila.

loosely disallied Immorally broke the alliance.

for that Because.

Capacity not raised Mental level not high enough.

affect Prefer. Grammatically linked to 'raised' in line 1028, but 'apt' should precede it.

Of constancy no roof infix'd Nothing planted in their character from which faithfulness could grow.

she The subject of this involved sentence.

a thorn intestine A domestic torment.

cleaving mischief Clinging force for evil.

his The single example of a husband is introduced by this possessive pronoun.

wreck Suffer shipwreck. This intransitive use is obsolete.

Steers-mate Steersman, subject to pilot's orders. Not the co-pilot of today.

who finds ... found Is he who finds that rarity, a virtuous wife. The moral reputation of the Restoration period has never stood high.

virtue ... most shines ... above The less fortunate husband, who still manges to control his would-be errant wife, is more admired in heaven.

least confusion The minimum of disturbance.

1061–1267

The Chorus looks for no flattering tongue in the next visitor, the giant Harapha, but wonders what his purpose can be in arriving with a frown but unarmed.

Harapha proclaims himself and expresses regret that he had never had the opportunity of a contest with Samson when the latter still had his eyesight. Challenged by Samson to try here and now, he boasts of what he would have done to Samson in a victory of which his opponent's blindness has robbed him.

Challenged again, he refuses to fight one who is not only blind but dirty.

Samson blames his condition on enemies too cowardly to meet him on the battlefield. He offers to fight Harapha, armed only with an oak staff, against everything with which the other can equip himself, provided the space is enclosed to compensate for his blindness.

Harapha protests that to offer such odds Samson must be

dependent on some magic power, which lay behind the pretence of his strength residing in his hair. Samson angrily maintains that his strength is not magic but the gift of God, and goes on to challenge Dagon to defeat what Harapha calls witchcraft, and what he knows as divine power.

With a sneer Harapha asks what help a god can give who has abandoned his champion to the tender mercies of his enemies, a contemptible opponent in greater need of shaving than swordplay. Accepting these insults as no more than he has deserved, Samson again invites single combat, to decide whose god is the real one.

Harapha finds further occasion for scorn in describing the would-be champion of the Israelite God as a murderer, revolter and robber, as proved when the men of Judah handed him over. To this Samson replies: (1) that his marriage to the Philistine woman of Timna resulted in a very unfriendly forcing from her of the answer to his riddle and the loss of his stake – which he naturally recovered for himself; and (2) that it is right to use force against a conqueror. It was wrong for his countrymen to extradite their heaven-sent champion as a common criminal. Once more, he offers a fight, a small undertaking for such a warrior as Harapha.

After a fierce exchange of threats – of what Samson will do to Harapha and of what Harapha will have others do to Samson – the Philistine departs, leaving the Hebrews to guess the outcome. The Chorus fear further affliction of their hero, but he suggests that Harapha will not, for shame, report the incident; and that his own labour is too profitable for the Philistines to forgo by weakening him. Nevertheless, death at the hands of his enemies would be a friendly act. Whatever they impose, out of hatred for him, may – now that his strength has returned – prove a disaster to them.

retire Withdraw.
contracted Led to, brought about (a Latin expression).
riddling days A reference to the riddle of the lion and the bees, the answer to which was wheedled out of him.
Harapha This invented name was probably taken from Rapha, father of Goliath and four other giants. Rapha is a Hebrew word for 'giant'. (Samuel 21,16–22).
pile Bulk. Strictly, a large building.

wind This metaphor from ships (cf. the simile applied to Dalila, lines 714–9) is continued in 'carried' and 'fraught'.

less conjecture i.e. can guess less, or have less need to guess.

habit Clothing. Presumably Harapha carries no weapon.

fraught Cargo, i.e. purpose (obsolete: form of 'freight').

Og King of Bashan, killed by the Israelites.

Anak Father of giants, the Anakim.

Emims ... held See Deuteronomy 2,10–11 and Genesis 14,5. Emim is the Semitic plural, like *cherubim*.

thou know'st me ... known i.e. my fame is at least equal to yours.

listed field The lists in a tournament (an anachronism).

Gyves Leg-fetters.

the Mill Samson's labour was grinding corn.

prowess Valiant deeds.

recover'd Regained.

in thy hand Within your power.

assassinated Treacherously attacked.

Brigandine Coat of mail; a 'habergeon' was similar, for head and shoulders.

Vant-brass Armour on forearm.

Greaves Armour to protect shins.

Gauntlet Glove of mail.

A Weaver's beam The wooden cylinder in the loom, hence a very thick shaft. (Regularly used of a giant's spear.)

seven-times-folded i.e. made of seven layers.

chafed This word and 'ruffled' both mean 'angered'.

The pledge of my unviolated vow The guarantee that my vow was unbroken.

spread before him Unfold to him.

From thine i.e. coming from the Philistines.

Fair honour A fine compliment you pay!

Tongue-doughty Full of brave words.

League-breaker i.e. breaker of a treaty between the Israelites and the Philistines (made by the 'men of Judah', see Judges 15,10–11).

Askalon See Judges 14,19.

a Wife i.e. the woman of Timnath.

no foe But compare lines 222–6.

Politician Intriguing (an adjective).

thirty spies 'Companies' in Judges 14,11.

in their coin i.e. with Philistine sheets and garments.

appellant Challenger (a term from tournaments).

maim'd for high attempts Too injured for great feats.

of small enforce Requiring little effort.

Due Liable.

descant Comment (now only a musical term).

Baäl-zebub A particular form of the sun god Baäl (Jupiter of the Palestine nations), the 'Lord of the Flies' worshipped in Ekron. See 2 Kings 1,2).

unused Unaccustomed (to such insults).

van Vanguard. The meaning is 'start fighting'.

baffled Publicly disgraced, like a coward in a tournament.

structure Cf. 'pile', line 1069.

Astaroth Phoenician goddess of love, often associated with Baäl.

braveries Defiant utterances.

Giantship Mocking imitation of 'lordship'.

unsconsci'nable Excessively long (gigantic).

Goliah Goliath, slain by David.

intend advantage of Wish to profit by.

it may ... deed i.e. they who attempt to kill me may bring destruction on themselves as well (a presentiment?)

1268–1299

The Chorus reflects on two things: the great renewal of spirit among the oppressed righteous when an omnipotent God sends a deliverer to crush their enemies, and the individual exercise of patience, which delivers from tyranny by sheer endurance.

Armouries and Magazines i.e. stores of armour and weapons.

Either of these i.e. either victory in combat or triumph through endurance.

1300–1426

The Chorus warns Samson of an approaching officer, one who is unlikely to waste his time on long speeches.

The officer orders Samson to accompany him immediately in order to be fed and cleaned up for a demonstration of his strength before an assembly of all the local notables.

Samson at first points out that he is forbidden by Hebrew law to perform at a heathen religious ceremony. Then he enquires why, with so many entertainers at hand, they have to call upon a tired-out slave – and he refuses. Warned by the officer, he declares his conscience is not as debased as his body. he may be their drudge but never their jester; he repeats that he will not come. The officer departs, dropping a dark hint of punishment to come.

While the Chorus fears the worst, Samson protests that to comply would be to prostitute his newly restored divine strength to idol worship. He is prepared to earn his keep at the mill, but not to perform in honour of Dagon. To obey this command he may offend God; yet God may, in a good cause, excuse such attendance. Here he is aware of a premonition. He changes his mind and agrees to go, without dishonour to God, but rather braced for some great achievement or a final release in death.

The officer reappears to threaten him with being dragged to the assembly, and is gratified to hear of Samson's resolve. The lords might even consider setting him free! Uncertain of his reception by the Philistines, Samson recommends his fellow-tribesmen to stay behind. There will be nothing discreditable in whatever happens, but he bids them farewell.

quaint Elaborately carved.

voluble Quickly delivered (in contrast to today's meaning of glib fluency of speech).

Ebrews The older form of this ancient name of the Jews.

remark him Mark him out.

Antics Clowns. This list of entertainers is from contemporary England.

Regard thyself Take care.

Join'd Commanded.

what speed thy message needs The sarcasm extends to both of the contemporary meanings of 'speed' – swiftness and success.

stoutness Boldness.

cause to sorrow Giving further expression to his presentiment.

so requite Repay thus my restoration to God's favour.

Vaunting Proudly demonstrating.

unclean, profane These two epithets are respectively the Hebrew and the classical labels for what is forbidden by religious law.

in their civil power Under their authority as a community.

outward acts defile not The Chorus is still arguing for obedience to the command to perform.

the sentence holds The saying is valid.

dispense with Treat as special cases for exemption.

surmounts my reach Is more than I can imagine.

something extraordinary In two words the vein of dramatic irony has become unsubtle. The hero's increasing awareness of a gigantic climax, by approximating to the known outcome, intensifies the thrill of anticipation in the minds of the audience. Only the cynic might wonder if part of Samson's original purpose in becoming familiar with the Philistines was to study local architecutre for structural defects!

aught of presage Anything genuinely prophetic.

Engines Instruments.

hamper Shackle.

as So that.

pernicious Fatal.

for a life To save his life. This change from his earlier death wish is probably intended as a cover for his change of mind, to disarm suspicion.

if aught ... concern'd If in any way religious topics are introduced.

1427–1440

The Chorus calls on God to guide aright the departing champion, to send the angel of his birth to protect him with the fire from the altar of his visitation, and to fill him with the spirit that used to spur him on to great feats of strength.

spread his name great Spread the greatness of His name.
that Spirit ... Dan See Judges 13,25.
mortal seed i.e. any man.

1441–1758

Manoa, no longer bowed down with care, hastens to tell his friends how he has fared in negotiating a ransom. Some, those of the priestly party, scorned the suggestion; others, the moderates, seemed drawn by the offer of money, while a third section, more liberal in outlook, thought that punishment had gone far enough and Samson could well be freed – for a modest sum.

Interrupted by the distant roar of the populace at the sight of Samson, Manoa goes on to say he will contribute all he possesses to ransom his son. The Chorus comments that the usual filial care for parents has in this case been replaced by paternal care for a child. Manoa pictures Samson back at home, his strength steadily returning with his hair, and perhaps, miraculously, his eyesight restored. The Chorus are joining in the pleasure of such a prospect when the crash is heard, so embracing in its volume of sound that the Chorus, intuitively, imagine that the whole town has perished. Accepting Manoa's supposition, they even wonder if, with his sight restored, Samson is slaying all the inhabitants.

The little group waits fearfully for news, soon brought by a fellow tribesman. The Messenger, panting like a fugitive and still wide-eyed with horror at what he has witnessed, does his best to break the news of Samson's death along with the massacre of the Philistines. Manoa, forestalled by Death in the paying of the ransom, is told that Samson brought slaughter on himself as well as on his enemies by pulling down the building.

Pressed for details, the Messenger describes the semicircular theatre, with its vault supported by two main pillars, the entry of Samson, liveried and guarded, his feats of strength and, at the interval, his speech from between the pillars. Promising them the most amazing feat of all, the blind prisoner tugged until the whole roof collapsed.

The lengthy narrative is followed by a choral hymn of triumph in which the single voice of the spokesman gives place to a combined chant, first by the full Chorus, then by the two halves. The Chorus briefly sings of the fulfilment of Samson's mission in massive slaughter of God's enemies, achieved only by his own self-sacrifice; the first semi-chorus enlarges on the madness, inspired from above, which drove the Philistines to bring about their own destruction by forcing Samson to entertain them. The second semi-chorus compares him in a climax of strange similes to a terrifying 'dragon' raiding poultry up there on their perches, to an eagle bringing disaster out of a cloudless sky, and to the phoenix rising out of her own ashes to achieve fame.

Manoa breaks in with the more prosaic subject of funeral preparations. 'Nothing is here for tears'; Samson's heroic end has brought lamentation on a national scale to his enemies. First they must find his body and wash it clean; then Manoa will assemble all his kindred for the procession home, where a monument will be erected to which youths will resort for inspiration and which virgins will annually decorate with flowers.

The last word is spoken by the Chorus in a blend of the general and the particular: we may often doubt God's wisdom or feel the weight of his displeasure, but he brings victory in the end. Samson has succeeded as champion beyond the wildest expectations. This handful of faithful witnesses, sadder and wiser men, their emotions subdued, quietly disperses.

my inducement hither Which brought me here.

no will No desire.

The rest i.e. of his punishment.

dread Object of fear.

not wanting ... want nothing Not lacking him I shall desire nothing else.

wont Are accustomed (modern 'are wont').

had not permitted Would not have permitted. Construction is completed in line 1498 'were not'.

Not to sit idle Dramatic irony.

vain Empty.

thereon Springing from (those hopes).

as next Being nearest (of kin). Tribesmen of Dan.

dealing dole Spreading dolour, grief.

presumptuous to be thought Which it would be over-confident of us to imagine.

subscribe Support, assent.

rides post Travels at maximum speed (with post horses).

baits Tarries at an inn (for refreshment of travellers and horses).

too much concern'd i.e. as fellow-tribesmen of Samson.

here before thee i.e. heard before the Messenger's appearance.

to know what well I utter In order to understand fully what I am about to say.

the sum ... circumstance defer The essence first, details later.

be grief in surfeit i.e. be more sorrow than you can stomach.

by whom i.e. by whom have the Philistines been overwhelmed.

lessens ... sorrow i.e. lightens our grief. Assuming the victor must be alive.

speak them out 'News' was originally plural.

discharge i.e. from imprisonment.

windy Empty.

at variance with Into dispute with.

lastly At the end of his life.

Occasions Business affairs.

banks Benches (the original meaning).

Timbrels Tambourines (a biblical word).

Cataphracts Soldiers in full armour; if mounted, their horses were similarly protected.

Rifted Rent.

assay'd Attempted.

appear Antagonist Offer to compete with him.

arched roof Vaulting was probably not known in Canaan; Milton would assume it was.

nerves Muscles.

As with the force ... tremble As when mountains tremble (e.g. earthquakes) with the force of winds and waters pent (underground). A contemporary explanation.

massy Massive.

Not willingly i.e. the self-killing was not suicide (an offence).

necessity Fate, in the heathen sense.

sublime Elated.

regorged Gorged upon.

Chaunting Singing the praises of (archaic spelling).

preferring 'It' is understood.

living Dread Our God: object of (religious) dread; 'living' because idols are dead matter. Cf. 'dread' in line 1474.

Silo Shilo. The Ark was here from the time of Joshua to that of Samuel.

hurt Perverted.

Unweetingly importuned Unwittingly urged on.

their own ruin An echo of the Latin proverb, derived ultimately from Euripides, 'Whom the gods would destroy they first make mad'.

thought extinguished Regarded as done for.

From under ashes An anticipation of the phoenix simile, lines 1699–1707.

ev'ning Dragon This biblical creature could be a serpent, but more likely a jackal prowling in the evening.

Assailant ... roosts i.e. attacking the fowls roosting on their perches. A bold example of *hypallage* (see pp.21 and 103).

tame villatic Fowl Timid farmyard poultry. The Roman 'villa' was a large country estate.

His cloudless thunder i.e. Samson's thunderbolt, out of a clear sky (unexpectedly), descended on them (like an eagle pouncing on its prey). In these two lines we have a *simile*, a *metaphor* and another case of *hypallage*.

virtue, given for lost i.e. his physical strength taken by his enemies for useless.

Depress'd Struck down.

self-begotten bird The Phoenix (a Greek word from the same root as 'Phoenician') was a fabulous bird of fine plumage. Every five hundred years it burnt itself to death, only to rise, a new creature, from its ashes. Usually regarded as belonging to an Arabian legend, it was placed by Herodotus in the Egyptian desert. In any case, a wood in the English sense would seem out of place. 'Embost' means in the midst of a bush, which *could* be a single palm tree.

no second knows no third Roundabout way of saying 'is unique'.

Holocaust A whole burnt offering at the altar. A Greek word for a Hebrew practice.

her ashy womb The ashes of her previous incarnation (the bird is variously male and female – here female as a symbol of Virtue).

teem'd Born, brought forth.

Revives The subject is Virtue, line 1697. It repeats 'roused his fiery virtue', line 1690. Lyrical outpourings are not tied by orderly arrangement. In these last four lines the literal Virtue and the figurative Phoenix are blended.

When most unactive deem'd Cf. line 1688.

body . . . fame This Phoenix-like personification of Virtue essentially refers to Samson.

secular Lasting for centuries (Latin 'seculum', a century).

ages of lives i.e. many generations.

Come, come The impatient Manoa has indeed had time to shed his tears and recollect his faculties after the shattering news. By nature, too, we may guess he had less time for dithyrambs than for elaborate funeral preparations.

Sons of *Caphtor* The Philistines are believed to have invaded, from Crete, the coastal area of Canaan.

freedom The Israelites were yet to suffer at the hands of the Philistines.

not parted from i.e. still favouring.

lavers Vessels for washing (from the French).

silent obsequy Funeral rites were, according to Hebrew custom, observed in silence by mourners.

unsearchable dispose Unfathomable planning.

best found in the close Discerned more clearly in the conclusion.

hath in . . . Bore witness Has on this very spot borne witness. The change to perfect tense marks the 'champion' in this case as Samson, as distinct from the general meaning in lines 1749–50.

band them Form themselves into a league.

new acquist Fresh acquisition.

all passion spent i.e. emotionally exhausted and at peace.

Questions

The minor poems

1 Write an appreciation of Milton's use of nature in these poems.

2 How far do you think the mythology employed by Milton enhances the poetic effect?

3 Find alternative titles for *L'Allegro* and *Il Penseroso*, and justify them. If you had to make a choice, which of the two would you prefer?

4 What features distinguish *Lycidas* as a pastoral poem?

5 Illustrate Milton's use of (a) colourful epithet, (b) musical phrase.

6 How many facets of the poet's character have you detected in his sonnets?

7 Which two sonnets, excluding those on the Massacre and on his blindness, do you like best? Give your reasons.

8 Choose three passages (maximum 20 lines) and say why you particularly like them.

9 Passages for paraphrase: *Lycidas*, 113–125, *Comus*, 18–36, Sonnet to Cromwell.

10 Find from these poems examples of as many different figures of speech as you can.

11 Summarize the argument of Comus against chastity and that of the Lady in favour of it.

12 Distinguish between the two brothers in *Comus*.

13 What weaknesses do you find in (a) the plot, (b) the characters in *Comus*.

14 Describe how you would produce *Comus*. Would you stage it indoors or outdoors?

15 If Milton were writing poetry today, what subjects do you think would attract his attention?

Samson Agonistes

16 Show how events were destined to lead up to the destruction of the Philistines.

17 In what spirit does Samson look back on his past actions, and what blame does he attach to others?

18 Indicate, with quotations from his speeches, the progressive effect on Samson of his dialogues with Manoa, Dalila and Harapha.

19 What did Milton and Samson have in common, and in what ways did they differ?

20 Illustrate Milton's use of dramatic irony in the play.

21 Outline the part played by the Chorus.

22 Quote some examples of effective repetition and explain the purpose in each case.

23 Find three apt similes and relate them to their context.

24 As a producer how would you deal with the end of the play, from line 1540 onwards?

25 Write an essay on Milton's choice of words and phrases.